# Pet Owner's Guide to
# THE
# SHETLAND SHEEPDOG

# Mary Davis

RINGPRESS

Published by Ringpress Books Limited,
Spirella House, Bridge Road,
Letchworth, Herts, United Kingdom, SG6 4ET.


First Published 1994
© 1994 Ringpress Books Limited.
All rights reserved

**ISBN 0 948955 98 8**


Printed and bound in Hong Kong

# Contents

*The long-coated Shetland Sheepdog, with its delightful expression, appeals to dog lovers all over the world.*

*Photography: Carol Ann Johnson*

# About the author

**Mary Davis** has been involved with Shetland Sheepdogs for more than forty years, and is universally acknowledged as a leading expert in the breed. She breeds, shows and judges Shelties, and has made up eight Champions, including the Working Group winner at Crufts. Mary is an International Championship Show judge, and has travelled to the United States, Canada, Australia, New Zealand, and most European countries on judging appointments, as well as judging the breed at Crufts. Mary is President of the English Shetland Sheepdog Club, and writes the breed notes for the UK's weekly dog paper, *Dog World*.

***Cover picture: Landover Black Flame (pet name Charlie),
owned by Kelly Forrest and Reg Perry.***

# Chapter One

# ORIGINS OF THE BREED

## THE SHETLAND ISLANDS

There is something legendary about Shetland – the most remote part of the British Isles – it lies so far north that it even resisted the Romans. They feared that the uncharted territory which lay beyond Orkney could be Ultima Thule - the Edge of the World. So perhaps it is not surprising that legends have attached themselves to the Shetland Sheepdog. The more you delve into the breed's background, the less likely it seems that the Sheltie was ever a sheepdog strictly in the herding sense of the word, and its name has been the subject of many misunderstandings over the years.

The Picts were the first inhabitants of Shetland, but the islands' documented history really began when the Norsemen settled, bringing their laws, customs, language and their fishing and farming way of life. They brought their livestock, too, including cattle, ponies, sheep and dogs. They governed Shetland for four hundred years, and when their authority was removed, it was not by force but by treaty. As a result, much of their influence, place-names, customs and traditions have remained.

## THE TOONIE DOG

Shetland has always been a land of tiny crofts or 'toons', which were grouped quite closely in any coastal areas offering shelter, safe beaches and a little arable land. They were protected by stone walls from the livestock which grazed on the surrounding hills. This was common land on which sheep and ponies were left as far as possible to fend for themselves.

The amount of herding involved in this type of husbandry was minimal, so the closest and most frequent contact between dogs and sheep would probably occur when wind and weather breached the protective stone walls. Any gap would be speedily exploited by an opportunist band of foraging sheep. Then the Toonie dog's job was to chase the invaders back to the hills. He performed the same function when the small crops had been harvested, and the sheep had been allowed in to glean the remnants.

Although described somewhat unflatteringly by one historian as a 'scavenger', the Toonie dog seems to have insinuated himself into the family, organising his little sleeping place in a corner of the cottage which he would, doubtless, guard with enthusiasm. He was a nondescript little creature. The likelihood of in-breeding, which would have stabilized some sort of type, was lessened by occasional, but close contact with dogs of various breeds which accompanied ships from all the North Sea countries from Iceland to as far south as Holland. To all these people, Shetland was a staging post and market place. To their dogs, it probably offered a welcome change of scene and company.

## THE INFLUENCE OF THE BORDER COLLIE

A less accidental influence occurred when the policy of land clearance and enclosure (which had already changed the economy and ecology of mainland Scotland) spread to Shetland. These activities established extensive sheep-runs to accommodate large flocks of imported sheep, and these really did need to be worked by purpose-bred sheepdogs of the Border Collie type. Both intentionally and accidentally no doubt, these dogs influenced the Toonie dogs, the results being clearly seen in the founding fathers of what eventually became the Shetland Sheepdog.

## THE BREED SPREADS

The next development accompanied the advent of tourism to Shetland. This established quite a tidy little trade in dogs which summer visitors took home with them. The breed became fairly well established on the Scottish mainland and inevitably, interest spread to the south of England, the first Shelties appearing at English Championship shows in about 1906. The breed had already been seen at Shetland agricultural shows, but now exhibitors were beginning to travel all over the British Isles. In 1909 some of the same dogs – several from Shetland – were seen at the Dundee Show in April, and at the Ladies' Kennel Association in London a few weeks later, before returning North for the Edinburgh Show.

Interest was spreading farther afield, too. Quite a large number of dogs and bitches went to America from about 1910, some, doubtless, direct from Shetland, others, through Mrs Ashton Cross, who, besides owning the world-famous Alderbourne Pekingese, ran a rather smart dog-shop in London, not far from the Ritz Hotel. Her daughter, Marjorie, actually bred a couple of litters of Shelties; one from each went to New York. Shelties very soon appeared in the American show ring, and in fact the first Champion of the breed, Lerwick Rex, gained his American title in 1915, a few weeks before Clifford Pat became the breed's first Champion in Britain.

## DRAWING UP A BREED STANDARD

The increasing respectability of the breed led to the formation of breed clubs in Shetland (1908), Scotland (1909) and England (1914). The Breed Standards of all three Clubs were very similar, all requiring the general type to resemble that of a Collie, the only problem being that each had in mind a different type of Collie. This, and the differing views of individual breeders, led to endless controversy for many years, but it was inevitable that Rough Collie crosses would eventually take place. While these crosses (some officially declared, and others strictly unofficial) ensured many problems over size and type, such short-cuts achieved success in a shorter time and to a higher standard than the original pioneers had imagined possible.

It is sad that during this era of progress, the links with the Toonie dogs were gradually broken. Breed pedigree charts show how swiftly the Collie crosses gained impetus and swamped the influence of the 'great' dogs of the past. But it is good to realise that many of the breeds which influenced the early bloodlines must have contributed to the versatility of the Sheltie of today. There is no need to regret that he is a sheepdog in name only. The Breed Standard ensures that he will always

*The Toonie Dog: The Shetland Sheepdog's ancestor was originally used to chase foraging sheep back into the hills.*

*The working sheepdog had to work over rough terrain in the harsh northern climate, and so the breed developed a warm, protective coat and an agile, athletic build.*

*The Sheltie's glamorous good looks have ensured its increasing popularity as a show dog and as a companion dog.*

retain the sound construction of a worker, and versatility is a lot easier to live with than the specialised demands of a specialised working dog.

The Sheltie's steady popularity is based on his willing adaptability, and on the fact that his beauty owes little to artifice. You do not have to be an expert trainer to own an obedient companionable Sheltie, neither do you need to be the Groomer of the Year to keep him looking a picture of glamour.

## THE SHELTIE
But how did the Shetland Sheepdog become known as the Sheltie? Far from being an affectionate diminutive acquired during recent times, this appears to be a name he borrowed long ago from the Shetland Pony, whose claim probably goes back to the beginning of the story. One of the Norse names for Shetland was *Hjaltland*. Say *'Hjalti'* as you fancy a Norseman would have done, and Sheltie owners all over the world will understand you perfectly!

# Chapter Two

# CHOOSING A PUPPY

**THE RIGHT BREED**
Before choosing an individual puppy, it is important to be quite sure that you have chosen the right breed. Every enthusiast thinks his breed is best, and certainly when it comes to totting up the pros and cons of the dog best-suited as a constant companion, the Sheltie must be very near the top of the poll. However, just as breeds of dog vary in type and temperament, so do people and every individual has a preferred lifestyle and a wide range of different tastes.

**CHARACTERISTICS OF THE SHELTIE**
Physically, the Sheltie is a most attractive dog. The breed is characterised by flowing lines, the profuse but well-fitting coat with its wide variations of colour, swift, neat movements, refined head and sweet expression, which all appeal to the average person's sense of natural beauty. What is more, all these attributes apply to all Shelties to a considerable degree, so that (with the exception of the hypercritical specialist) the average companion Sheltie can be as beautiful as the top show dog.

The Sheltie's mental reactions are as quick as his movements, and the breed is extremely biddable, being genuinely anxious to please. Compared with more independent breeds, the Sheltie is totally free from any wish to challenge or defy his owner. His natural inclination is to obey.

There is a reverse side to every coin, so what are the drawbacks to the Sheltie as a companion? The long coat has to be cared for and, of course, it does shed, sometimes a little at a time, but at least once a year in a thorough moult, which needs to be dealt with by equally thorough grooming. This is not quite as bad as it sounds, as unlike the average short-coated breeds, Sheltie hair does not penetrate carpets or upholstery. Instead, it lies on the surface so that it is easily cleaned from small areas with a damp sponge or a purpose-made brush. The vacuum cleaner removes it very efficiently from carpets.

The Sheltie's quick reactions and his protective instincts make him a very vigilant house dog. His bark is bigger than his size, and his keenness to demonstrate this fact can be a plus or a minus sign, depending on circumstances. The Sheltie used to be regarded almost exclusively as a country dog, often living an idyllic but very secluded life, which intensified the breed's natural reserve toward strangers. However, growing popularity has introduced him to a wider, busier world, which his trust in his owner enables him to accept. Nowadays, a sensibly reared puppy will usually adapt himself happily to any normal surroundings. Although still primarily a one-family dog, the Sheltie does not regard every stranger with dark suspicion. Neither does he

*ABOVE: The coat you see at eight weeks is only puppy-fluff, and gives little indication of the adult coat.*

*LEFT ( and opposite):Blue merle is a specialist's colour. A dog may have dark-brown eyes, blue eyes, or one of each, with this colour.*

ABOVE: A tri-colour and a sable showing the full adult coat. Both colour and length of coat change with maturity. Blue merles should never be mated to sables, nor (except by very experienced breeders) to other blue merles. The best mating for a merle is to a tricolour.

fawn on strangers. Always alert and never lethargic, he usually reacts in a very positive way to pleasure or alarm.

The Sheltie is naturally gregarious with other dogs, especially those of his own breed. He usually likes and invariably tolerates cats and other domestic pets while being easily trained to respect farm animals. The Sheltie is no Toy, but he is small enough to be acceptable anywhere, being very quiet and unobtrusive in surroundings which he does not feel called upon to protect. This is a dog that will enjoy any amount of exercise; he is the ideal country companion, happy to stir up the rabbits, but unless encouraged, he is seldom a confirmed hunter.

Most importantly, the Sheltie's small size and air of refinement should not be interpreted as a tendency to delicacy. This is a tough, long-lived breed, and although the Sheltie will happily live in the lap of luxury, posing as an ornament to any home, he is still basically an outdoor type, needing a sensible diet, lots of exercise and above all, the constant companionship of an understanding and appreciative owner.

## FINDING A BREEDER

There are sound reasons for suggesting that a puppy of any breed should be bought from a reputable breeder. The advantage is that you will have an opportunity to see the whole litter. The breeder will be on hand to give you all the information you need, and most breeders are only too happy to follow this up with a very valuable long-term after-sales service.

How can such a breeder be contacted? The best way is to call or write to your national Kennel Club, and you will be supplied either with a list of breeders or the name of the secretary of your local breed club, who will put you in touch with Sheltie breeders who live in your locality. Some breed clubs run puppy registers, which list puppies currently for sale, usually indicating the age, sex and colour available.

Of course, you can visit any or all of the kennels that you are put in touch with. However, it is not very advisable to embark on a one-day kennel crawl, as the majority of the puppies you see will be very vulnerable to infection. It is much better to allow yourself time between visits, and this will also give you a chance to evaluate what you have seen. You may not have to shop around at all. The first breeder contacted may sound helpful and understanding, and may have a likely puppy for sale.

There is no need to rush out and buy expensive beds, bowls or toys, let alone collars and leads, before you buy your puppy. They may well prove to be unsuitable. You may not even have to buy food in advance. The breeder will explain the puppy's needs and, if necessary, provide a sample meal.

## MALE OR FEMALE

Some people have an open mind on whether they want a male or female. However, the majority of pet owners express a preference for a female, believing that they are cleaner, more affectionate, easier to train and less likely to wander. In fact there is very little difference in character between the two sexes. The male has all the pleasing attributes of the bitch, plus the obvious advantage of not having to cope with the bitch's seasonal cycle.

The male is often easier to house train, and he seems to have an extra touch of individuality. He can be even more beautiful than the female with that extra wealth of coat and abundant mane giving a particularly distinguished look. The male Sheltie does not have a great wanderlust, and is most unlikely to set out in search of adventure. So unless you plan to get involved in breeding, when you will certainly want to start off with a bitch, it is worth keeping an open mind on which sex to choose.

## COLOUR

Shelties comes in four colours: sable, tricolour, black-and-white, and blue merle, all with white markings. Some people have set ideas as to which colour they prefer. In my experience, sable and white is the most popular choice. However, colour can be most deceptive, and if you choose a sable puppy you will have to take a good deal on trust.

The coat you see at eight weeks will only be temporary puppy-fluff, and at this age even the youngster that will finish a bright golden sable may look rather washed out. Do not look too unfavourably on that mouse-coloured pup if the breeder assures you that within a few weeks it will start blossoming to a brilliant copper or deep red-gold. The owlish dark spectacles will fade and make way for an attractive widow's peak. A shaded sable with darker frills framing its face can produce the most beautiful of Sheltie expressions. A rather sombre tricolour will look much smarter when the rather wishy-washy markings brighten to a rich tan.

Blue merle is something of a specialist's colour. At its best it can be the most beautiful, at its worst it is the least attractive of Sheltie colours. At eight weeks, a 'good' blue merle (which will develop into the right colour) may be very pale. The background colour may be tinted with just enough milky-blue to distinguish the body colour from the white of the collar and legs. The black markings should be flecks rather than patches. There may or may not be tan markings on the eyebrows, legs etc. Don't forget that while the merle may have two dark-brown eyes, two blue eyes are equally correct, as are 'odd' eyes (one brown, one blue), or both eyes may be brown flecked with blue. In any other colour than merle, only two brown eyes are correct.

In all four Sheltie colours, the white markings tend to shrink in extent as the puppy grows. So a wide white face blaze may finish as a narrow one, while a narrow blaze will probably vanish. Any white marking on the body itself (apart from the neck) is a serious show fault though a so-called mis-marked puppy is perfectly acceptable (it may even be exceptionally smart) as a pet.

With all the variations of shades and marking, there is quite a wide choice of colours. The only one which would be quite unacceptable is a wholly (or almost entirely) white puppy, bred from two blue merle parents. It could have seriously defective sight and/or hearing. Happily, the chance of your being offered such a puppy is virtually nil.

## ASSESSING THE PUPPIES

Do not be offended if your own credentials are carefully checked by the breeder before a sale is agreed. A responsible breeder will want to ensure that you are not buying the puppy for resale, that you have a suitably enclosed garden, and that there is somebody at home all day (you will be allowed an hour or two off to do the shopping!). On both sides, first impressions count a lot. Hopefully, the breeder will be quickly reassured that you will be a suitable owner. For your part, a quick glance

*ABOVE: By eight weeks old, the litter will be fully weaned.*

*LEFT: A puppy should look bright-eyed, healthy and clean.*

*ABOVE: It takes a very experienced breeder to assess how a Sheltie puppy is going to turn out.*

*RIGHT: Temperament is as important as appearance, and the Shetland Sheepdog should always be friendly and confident.*

round should tell you that the premises are clean, tidy and pleasant, indicating that the kennels are well-run, and the puppies are well cared for.

Buying and selling a living creature is more than a financial transaction. On both sides, it should be a commitment for the life of that particular animal. The purchaser should be able to guarantee a good, suitable, permanent home with proper care and attention. The seller should provide adequate advice to this effect, and should make it clear that in the case of a drastic change in the purchaser's circumstances, help would be available in re-homing the dog.

If the litter is allowed the freedom to play outside, it is not easy to keep puppies absolutely spotless for long. However, the self-respecting breeder will have made every effort to achieve this. The healthy puppy will not only look clean, but will feel sleek to the touch. It will seem plump without being grossly fat or pot-bellied. When you pick up a puppy it should feel just a bit heavier than it looks. A puppy which feels surprisingly light, even though it may not be noticeably skinny, may lack bone substance or be a 'poor doer'. The skin should never feel gritty to the touch – this may suggest fleas. These are easy enough to get rid of, but they simply should not be there.

Temperament is at least as important as looks, and at eight weeks the puppy should be quite happy to be placed in your arms and cuddled, However, if he soon decides he wants to join his littermates, playing around your feet, never mind. Make sure the puppy does not try to jump out of your arms, and if you have children, watch carefully to make sure that a pup is not accidentally dropped. Think twice (very hard!) about the puppy that struggles in panic rather than excitement, or one that goes rigid with apprehension when placed on your lap.

The recommendation about seeing the mother with her puppies can be slightly exasperating for the breeder, as Sheltie bitches look far from their best after rearing a litter. So if, at your request, a somewhat tatty-looking, homely body is ushered in, do not conclude that this simply cannot be the Champion, whose photograph you so admired. She will probably have very little hair on her underside, precious little on her tail, while most of her petticoats will have been cut off; a customary and wise precaution taken immediately before a long-haired bitch is due to whelp.

The genuine breeder will be happy to go over the puppy with you, explaining the various breed points while giving you a fair idea how it is likely to grow up as regards size etc. Don't expect to see an adult in miniature – Sheltie puppies are among the most difficult to evaluate at an early age, and it takes a lot of experience to forecast the eventual outcome with any degree of accuracy. Heads in particular change enormously, and at eight weeks or so the head is relatively short and chunky. A lovely long, Collie-type head (especially if accompanied by heavily-boned legs and knobbly knees) suggests eventual oversize.

If you have absolutely no intention of breeding from your bitch puppy, on no account should you allow yourself to be talked into an agreement to do so. Tempting as it may be to be offered a really good puppy at a reduced price on 'breeding terms', changed circumstances might make it difficult for you to fulfil the requirements, and at worst you could find yourself committed to a great deal of worry and expense.

If you are buying a male, it is as well to ask whether he is apparently 'entire' – i.e. that he has two readily detectable testicles in approximately the right place for his age. So-called monorchids – males with only one testicle descended (more correctly uni-lateral cryptorchids) are by no means unknown in Shelties, probably because a number of famous stud dogs of the past were what is popularly called 'mons'. The fault is almost certainly hereditary, so it continues to crop up from time to time. Shelties are also notoriously apt to mature late in this respect. A non-entire puppy makes an acceptable pet, but it is better to know the facts before having them pointed out to you by the vet when you take the pup to be inoculated. Talk things over with the breeder.

You should enquire whether your puppy (together with the rest of the litter) has been tested for Collie Eye Anomaly, and there is no reason why you should not ask to see the relevant certificate. In fact, you may be given a copy. (See Chapter Eight: Health Care). If the puppy is mildly affected there is seldom cause for the slightest alarm.

## COLLECTING YOUR PUPPY

When you go to collect your puppy you will almost certainly be given a sheet of useful information giving the puppy's present and future feeding requirements. It may offer many other hints on rearing and general care. You should also be given a copy of your puppy's pedigree, together with the registration certificate, duly signed by the breeder. You should forward this certificate with the necessary fee to the Kennel Club so that the registration of the puppy may be transferred to your name. The breeder's information sheet will almost certainly conclude with the request that you should keep in touch with the breeder, whose interest in the puppy will not cease with the receipt of your cheque.

One particularly important point is that, should it ever become necessary to find a new home for the puppy, you should contact the breeder immediately. For a responsible breeder, it is very distressing to hear through a breed rescue organisation that one of your dogs has to be re-homed, simply because the owner has been too embarrassed to admit this necessity to the breeder – the person most concerned and best able to help. There is no need for embarrassment, but there is every reason for contact to be maintained.

If you are travelling by car, make sure you have a responsible adult who can hold the puppy, and make sure you bring a towel for the puppy to lie on, and some paper towelling, in case of any accidents.

*It is important to ensure that your Sheltie is given every chance to settle down in his new home.*

# Chapter Three

# CARING FOR YOUR SHELTIE

## PREPARING YOUR HOME
Although you may have previously kept a dog – even another Sheltie – in your home for years without incident or accident, it is a good idea to check fences, hedges and gates for one hundred per cent security before collecting your new puppy. Chicken-wire can become rusted or torn, and hedges may have become bare, allowing room for a small puppy to find a way through. It is a good idea to have spring hinges and automatically closing latches fitted to all gates, and do make sure the pup cannot get under or through the front gate.

If the garden is not separately fenced from the drive leading to the garage, make sure the drive gates are also puppy-proof. Unless you own a lot of land, it is advisable to have the back and front gardens separated from one another by gates or by solid fencing. Shelties are not predisposed to wander from their homes – quite the reverse – but young puppies are naturally inquisitive and can squeeze through the most improbably small spaces.

If you have just moved to a brand-new house, it might be better to wait for a while before buying a new puppy – just until yards of chain-link have been screened by shrubs or by more secure fencing. The very young puppy is not likely to be noisy, but if he is offered an unobstructed 360 degree view of the great wide world, a youngster old enough to recognise his own territory may be too keen to tell you that the milkman is coming up the road or that the dog next door has been saying rude things through the fence.

## ARRIVING HOME
It is advisable to arrange to collect your puppy in the middle of the day, so he has a chance to settle into his new home before nightfall. In your own interests, try to be as punctual as possible, as careful arrangements will have been made about withholding your puppy's breakfast or giving him a travel pill. By collecting him reasonably early in the day you will have the best opportunity of easing him into his new home with a minimum of upset. Settling your puppy into his new home is a matter of commonsense. If the puppy is to spend a lot of time in the kitchen, you will obviously ensure that no electric cords are left trailing on the floor, the contents of any open shelves must be out of reach, and no plastic bags or any other 'chewable' or potentially dangerous objects should be left lying around.

## FEEDING
The breeder will have provided a diet sheet, and it makes sense to stick rigidly to this

for at least a couple of weeks, or until the puppy has outgrown the instructions. The diet I use at eight weeks is based on approximately 2ozs chopped (minced) raw beef, one-third to half a pint of milk, plus carbohydrate and suitable vitamin/mineral supplement, fed as follows:

BREAKFAST: Cereal (such as wheat flakes) soaked in half the daily ration of warmed milk in which a half teaspoonful of honey has been dissolved.
LUNCH: Half the daily ration of chopped beef with a sprinkling of comprehensive vitamin/mineral supplement, plus enough very fine wholemeal puppy-meal soaked in stock or gravy to achieve a crumbly (but not sloppy) consistency.
SNACK: As breakfast, but without the honey.
SUPPER: (Fed very shortly before your bedtime). As lunch, but without the supplement.

The reason the last meal is given so late is that within a few minutes the pup will relieve himself. After he has performed both functions (hopefully on the paper provided), replace the paper. Then encourage the puppy into his bed with a few small, hard biscuits, switch off the light and make a quick getaway. For the first night or two (until he gets his bearings) put plenty of paper very near his bed, gradually moving it nearer the door.

## THE DEVELOPING PUPPY
The meat should be increased gradually until at three months the pup is getting 3-4ozs a day. Milk does not need to be increased, and it can be omitted if it is not quickly cleaned up. It may be helpful to try diluted evaporated milk, which the puppy may have been weaned on. The meat will not need to be minced, and it can be varied in type to include canned food, remembering that fatty, over-rich or sloppy food – or too much of anything – can upset a Sheltie's digestion.

By four months, meals can be reduced to three by omitting the afternoon snack and feeding supper earlier in the evening. By five months the puppy should be getting the adult meat ration of about 6ozs (170g.) – more or less, depending on size and appetite – together with three heaped tablespoonsful of soaked wholewheat puppy-meal, still divided into two meals. The morning milk (if still unpopular) can be replaced by a token breakfast of hard, dry, crunchy biscuit. The chosen supplement should be continued until one year, and then only given at times of need (e.g. when the dog is changing his coat).

The adult Sheltie needs only one meal a day (early evening is a usually a convenient time), but he will still enjoy a token breakfast of dry hound-meal and a bed-time snack of a small biscuit or two

## DIET VARIATIONS
As already mentioned, canned food may be given. The best and most suitable (also one of the most expensive!) will be that containing the least jelly or gravy. Cans are a most useful standby, especially at holiday time – nowadays you do not even have to remember to pack the can-opener!

Frozen meats can be obtained (from animal feed stores or pet-shops) in a wide variety. Beef, lamb, liver and ox-cheek are available in chunks or even more conveniently in one-pound (425g.) minced packs, as are chicken, turkey, rabbit or tripe. Free-flow packs are particularly convenient. Household scraps (vegetables, fish, etc.) chopped and added to the soaked biscuit meal are always welcome, but they seldom add up to a square meal.

## COMPLETE DIETS
These have grown enormously popular in recent years, and there are many different brands available. They are well-named 'convenience' foods, as all the hard work is done for us. As well as the staple nourishment, all the extras in the way of vitamins, minerals and trace elements are incorporated in ideal balance. Nothing should be added to the complete diet, as this will upset the balance. This is, perhaps, a mixed blessing as it is sometimes difficult for the owner to accept the infallibility of these scientific formulae. Commonsense should tell us that no dog food will be marketable unless dogs eat it readily. So at least as much research must have been expended on making the food palatable as on making it nourishing. However, unless an equal amount of research is directed at making it visually appealing to the human eye, owners will continue to add a bit of this and that to add interest to an apparently boring meal – and bang goes the balance!

Although the packaging of complete foods advises that fresh water must always be available, some brands do not give detailed advice as to whether the food should be fed dry or soaked. The degree to which some such foods (including mixers) can expand when soaked is positively amazing. Since Shelties have a tendency to kidney trouble (especially in old age), I find this a cause for concern, and that is why I prefer the traditional meat and biscuit diet.

## WHAT TO BUY

### BEDS AND BEDDING
The most practical bed for a young puppy is a very stout cardboard or lightweight wooden box, with a conveniently placed door cut in it to exclude draughts and retain bedding. This will be outgrown so quickly, it is not worth buying a dog bed at this stage. For the first few nights  some pieces of blanket or similar woollen material will provide a cosy, nest-like bed. Such material easily rumples up and gets torn and soiled, so as soon as possible it should be replaced by a piece of synthetic fleece material.

The chances are that the pup will have been reared on this bedding which is strong and easy to wash. It is much firmer than a blanket, it tends to lie flat, it is less likely to be chewed, and any moisture is shed through its tough backing. So, if there is a chance of accidents, several layers of newspapers should be placed underneath and removed at frequent intervals.

### PERMANENT BEDS
By far the most practical dog bed is the tough, plastic type, which is oval in shape so as to avoid dust-trapping corners, and is big enough to allow the dog ample room to lie flat as well as to curl up. Again, the synthetic fleece material makes the best bedding.

The traditional wicker baskets are totally impractical as they are real dust-traps, and they are virtually impossible to clean properly. The wicker is irresistible to puppy teeth and the resulting splintered ends are a hazard to dog and owner alike.

*The Sheltie is a lively, intelligent dog and will want to explore his new surroundings.*

*ABOVE: If you are feeding a complete diet, there is no need to add any extras.*

*RIGHT: Your puppy will need suitable toys to play with.*

Bean bags and dog duvets are attractive to look at, but both have drawbacks. Bean bags, though comfortable once the dog has overcome an initial wariness, are bound to leak sooner or later, and no matter how often you vacuum, there are always stray beads lurking in the corners. Both bean bags and duvets require really tough zipped spare covers. However, this does not provide a satisfactory solution, as a zip is the ultimate challenge to a Sheltie, and replacing zips can be an expensive business.

In America the use of indoor kennels is widespread, and these are now becoming increasingly popular in the UK and elsewhere. They can provide a safe haven for a puppy at times of hectic household activity and they can be a safeguard when travelling. However, no dog should be confined in a limited space for long periods, and it must always be remembered that the Sheltie is an active, energetic breed, not a lap dog.

## COLLARS

Debates over the desirability of micro-chips or tattoos for dogs may rage for some time to come, but meanwhile, a collar carrying means of identification is a cheap and obvious investment, as well as a mandatory obligation. Until lead training is completed, the most comfortable neck-wear for a young puppy is a soft, flexible cat-collar. For routine use, a fine, rolled leather collar is the most suitable. A thirteen inch (33cm) collar will fit the average-sized Sheltie. Wider, flat leather collars are neither safe nor suitable for this breed. Metal studs could catch in the hair.

A leather collar needs to be fitted right into the neck-hair and then manipulated until it is settled in securely. Rather like a horse's girth, the collar may have to be tightened a little after you think it is safely in place. A collar that is a little on the tight side is much safer than one that is too loose. A Sheltie's skull is very narrow, and a collar that can work up the neck will certainly slip over the head.

A choke chain is usually advised for Obedience training, but otherwise should not be used for any length of time or it will damage the neck-hair. The excessively heavy choke chain with enormous links is unsuitable for a Sheltie. Surprisingly, the lightweight nylon collar with a double choke chain addition, has a very gentle checking effect, and this can be very useful in a situation when a Sheltie could slip his head out of an ordinary collar. They can be adjusted by means of buckles, so they can be used with or without a lead.

## LEADS

Nylon or leather leads are equally suitable, but the lead should not be too narrow. A very lightweight lead, so useful in the show-ring, can easily slip through gloved fingers, especially in wet weather. A chain lead, even the type with a leather handle, is uncomfortable to use and quite unnecessary. It is much easier to train a Sheltie not to pull, or not to chew the lead, rather than having a couple of yards of chain wound round your hand.

Any type of lead is only as safe as the clip; security always being preferable to quick-release convenience in this respect. It is always worth examining clips from time to time, to check that they have not become rusty, worn or otherwise unsafe.

It is a good idea to carry in your pocket a lightweight nylon or leather lead with a ring instead of a clip on the end. This can be slipped over the dog's head in case of an emergency. Apart from the fact that legislation is constantly being strengthened in favour of closer control of dogs, a safe lead can be a lifeline. By the way, no self-respecting Sheltie would care to be seen in a harness!

## EXERCISE

The very young, newly-acquired puppy has no need for formal exercise, and in any case, he will be confined to the house and garden until fully protected by vaccination. Although your puppy will love to get involved in any activities going on around him, his capacity for play is limited by his need for plenty of rest, and he should not be tempted into activity once his energy has started to flag. If your puppy is encouraged to continue playing, he will not only become physically exhausted but may also become mentally bewildered.

The adult dog, however, can take lots of exercise. Regardless of any uncertainties about his original working background, the stipulations of the Breed Standard (the written blueprint of the breed) has always ensured that the Sheltie's conformation is free from exaggerations or abnormalities. The Sheltie is a dog capable of speed, activity and endurance.

In order to keep this sound structure in good muscular condition, and also to ensure that the Sheltie's alert mentality is not frustrated by boredom, daily exercise is an enjoyable necessity. A ten-minute stroll on the lead is only enough to encourage sloppy or restricted movement. To keep the muscles and ligaments in trim, the dog needs to use its natural paces – the brisk trot interspersed by the full-out gallop. Of course, a cross-country walk is ideal, but a feasible alternative is to team up with another Sheltie owner to enjoy communal trips to the nearest open space. Better still, why not invest in a second Sheltie? Anybody who does so agrees that the fun and enjoyment this brings far outweighs any extra expense. Nobody understands the Sheltie's play requirements better than another Sheltie, and they are great company for one another when left alone.

When exercising Shelties in public open spaces, you need to be watchful. The Sheltie is the least aggressive of creatures, but even the most equable Sheltie can be intimidated by a couple of excessively boisterous bigger dogs, and he will not relish being chased, even though the intent is well-meaning. In such a case, the Sheltie sees his only means of defence in flight, and once outside the physical and mental restraints of his owner, the Sheltie is prone to panic. A frightened Sheltie heading at speed toward the park gate sets the stage for a nasty scenario. So it is sensible to keep your dog close to your side when confronted in this way, despite any assurances that the other dogs only want to play.

When exercising dogs in open country it is far safer to avoid farmland or other private property. Apart from the possibility of disturbing stock or game, you may have no means of telling whether land, crops or trees have been sprayed or otherwise treated with chemicals. Even public footpaths are not necessarily safe, so use unfamiliar routes with caution. Luckily there are still plenty of unspoiled natural areas where it is safe and acceptable to walk dogs, but how long this will last depends to a great extent on the willingness of dog owners to accept responsibility for their pets. Some public authorities do their best to appease both dog-lovers and dog-haters by continuing to allow free access for dogs to beauty spots, while urging owners to use the facilities for cleaning up, or even preventing fouling by using exercising places provided in recreation areas. It is so depressing and embarrassing to see how often these concessions are ignored.

*A tough, plastic bed, fitted with comfortable bedding, is ideal for the Shetland Sheepdog.*

## DOGS AND CARS

Most dogs love going out in the car. The dog who loathes travelling is usually the one who has been thoughtlessly introduced to car travel by being slung in the back, without any provision being made for his comfort, security or reassurance, and whose tendency (natural in the circumstances) to car-sickness has not been noticed until it is too late.

A small puppy is obviously more comfortable when held on a passenger's lap. Even so, the puppy should wear a collar and lead so that he can easily be restrained in the case of a sudden stop or swerve, or if the door is unexpectedly opened. It is also advisable for the adult dog to wear a lead in the car as well as the obligatory collar and identity tag. There are two schools of thought about the use of the lead. It may be considered slightly risky in case the lead should become entangled in some fitting or fixture. However, this hazard is outweighed by the fact that a lead is easy to grab if the rear of the car is suddenly opened, while in the case of an accident, the lead makes immediate recapture of a loose dog much easier.

Nowadays the majority of show dogs (who cover thousands of miles a year) travel in cages. These can be removable or may be custom-made as an integral part of the car. They can be made very comfortable, offering maximum ventilation and observation, and they may be a safeguard in case of an accident. The average car-guard, unless it is made not only for the car but for the owner's specific purpose, can, at best, be regarded as a rather ineffective deterrent to a Sheltie, who will almost certainly be able to creep round or under some part of it.

The companion Sheltie must be trained to travel in whichever part of the car is most convenient. This is particularly important on long journeys, when you want your dog to settle down and travel in a relaxed, comfortable style. Above all, a

ABOVE: A puppy has no need of formal exercise for the first few weeks in his new home – he will be quite happy playing in the garden.

RIGHT: If your dog is going to travel a lot, it is advisable to buy a crate, which is a safe and comfortable method of transporting puppy or adult.

combination of a lead and the command "Stay", should be taught to make quite sure that the dog will not leap out as soon as the door is opened. *Never* let your Sheltie jump out unless you are there to take hold of the lead, and never release him until you have checked that it is safe to do so. This is particularly true if your Sheltie is not yet happy in the car – always make sure he is securely installed in the car before opening the drive gates, or he may take evasive action into the road!

When you are out for the day, always take care to park the car on the same side of the road that you intend starting out for a walk. If your dog gets lost, he will usually return to the car. This is fine, provided the dog does not have to cross the road to reach the car.

A car-sick dog is never going to be a happy traveller, let alone an agreeable one, so if car-sickness shows signs of becoming a problem, a suitable remedy should be tried. Your vet will suggest a suitable product to try. Make sure you follow the instructions, and give the right dosage, depending on the age and weight of your Sheltie.

A dog can become accustomed to car travel by going on lots of short trips, to and from somewhere suitable for a pleasant walk. This certainly makes sense, as the dog starts to associate the car with something that is enjoyable. However, for the very occasional 'hopeless' case the reverse may be effective. Take the dog on a very long ride – a couple of hundred miles, if possible – making him a really comfortable bed and giving him a walk on the way. The Sheltie may then realise that the car is a familiar refuge in a strange world, and he will probably travel back (the same day) without being sick at all. In such a case, the car sickness is obviously a nervous rather than a physical reaction, and after a couple of long trips your Sheltie will, hopefully, be hopping in and out of the car quite happily.

The risk of leaving dogs alone in cars cannot be stressed too strongly. On a seemingly cool day, it takes only a little sunlight to raise the inside temperature of a car to danger point. A hot summer day can turn a car into a death trap in a very short space of time. It is not a good idea to allow your Sheltie to hang his head out of the window as you drive along. Apart from the risk of injury in the case of even a minor accident, this sort of thing does no good to eyes or ears. If windows need to be kept open, whether the car is moving or stationary, they can be kept safe by the use of purposely-made pieces of expanding plastic trellis.

# Chapter Four

# TRAINING YOUR SHELTIE

The period when the new puppy is awaiting the completion of his inoculation programme is a splendid opportunity for dog and owner to establish a bond of understanding, and to start elementary but important aspects of training.

## VOCABULARY

Before reaching his new home, the puppy will have heard a wide range of soppy endearments, and he will also have some idea of the meaning of "In" and "Out", "Come" and "Stay". Rather regrettably, "No!" will be right at the top of the list.

I do not think it necessary, except in formal competitive situations, to bark commands at Shelties. Barking is for dogs, not people. However, although most owners normally use a conversational tone to ask a dog to "Come along in"or "Do go and lie down", and maybe "George, don't do that!", a firmer tone should be used for the single-word commands. It is particularly useful to choose one of these as a keyword, to be used only in an emergency.

"Stay" is very useful command, covering many situations, from the undignified scuffle in the doorway when the pup tries to get through first, to the potentially dangerous situation when a car door opens unexpectedly. So it might be a better idea to use "Back" for the doorway confrontation, and to save "Stay" for a true emergency, so that, recognising the urgency in your voice, the dog told to "Stay!" would freeze to the spot. That one word could be a lifeline.

## HOUSE TRAINING

As soon as you get your puppy home, let him have a quick look round the kitchen, followed by a more detailed exploration of the garden, where he might oblige. If he does, pick him up, praise him to the skies, take him indoors and give him the meal he probably missed in the interests of an uneventful journey. If he does not perform after a reasonable time, take him in, feed him and take him out again. This time you will probably have better luck.

For the first few nights it would be unreasonable to expect miracles, which is why the last meal should be given immediately before you go to bed. At this age (eight weeks or so) a puppy's bladder and bowel movements follow a meal very quickly, so that it is probable that he will use the paper which you have placed near his bed. When he does so, replace the paper and put some more by the door, praise him and drop a couple of small biscuits in his bed. The minute you get up in the morning, let him out and hope for the best – which is all you can reasonably do in the first few days. The puppy will perform after every meal and every time he wakes

*LEFT: Teaching the "Sit" is a basic requirement for the well-behaved dog.*

*RIGHT: The Sheltie is an intelligent dog and will be quick to learn.*

## TEACHING THE "DOWN"

*Tone of voice is all-important when giving the command "Down".*

*Hold your dog in the "Down" for a few seconds, giving plenty of praise.*

up from a sleep, so these are the times to be vigilant. If you invest in a puppy-run this may solve two potential problems. Firstly, a common hazard of using newspaper for house training is that the puppy gets so hooked on the paper that he will rush in from the garden to use it. Secondly, in view of the increasing public pressure against fouling, it is essential to encourage dogs to use their own gardens *before* going for a walk. These two aims should be compatible. If you install the run (complete with paper) in a spot that is easy for you to clean and obvious to the puppy, you could, hopefully, get him to use the garden rather than the kitchen or the great outside world. To begin with, he could be shut in the run until all is well. Eventually, your Sheltie should use the same place automatically, without the run.

An indoor kennel or crate can be used as an aid to house training. Newspapers are placed at one end of the crate, and the puppy will learn to use this end for toilet purposes rather than foul his own sleeping quarters. However, there is a risk that this habit might become instilled and therefore could be difficult to break as the puppy grows older.

## LEAD TRAINING

Many people prefer to accustom the puppy to wearing a collar prior to attaching the lead, but I prefer to start by using a show slipover with a sliding neckpiece. Not only can this be adjusted very quickly without a choking sensation, but it avoids the slightly alarming moment (for the puppy) when you would have to grasp the collar to clip on the lead.

The first time the puppy is put on the lead, he will probably resist, so it is best to start the lesson before a meal and to have a tidbit handy to coax him forward. It helps to have somebody else to do this, so that you can follow behind at a speed that will keep the lead slack. Puppies vary enormously in how quickly they learn to cooperate. The apparently sensible pup may prove the most reluctant, and the flighty one may take to the lead as a duck to water. Do not despair if your pup screams blue murder, leaps in the air, and then casts himself dramatically on the ground – he may be the first to capitulate.

There is no easy way  to teach this lesson. You just have to keep up an endless stream of chatter, coaxing the puppy forward, maybe inches at a time. Try to avoid unnecessary pressure on the lead, but be prepared to ignore resistance if all else fails. After the first lesson you may feel you have achieved nothing, but do not communicate this feeling to the puppy. After a few minutes tell the pup how clever he is, pick him up and cuddle him, and then take him indoors to give him his meal. Next day you may have to start from scratch, there may be a slight improvement or – wonder of wonders – he may trot on reasonably well. Even if it takes two to three lessons, success will come in the end, and then you can start regular practice.

The first thing the puppy has to learn is not to get under your feet. He should walk (or rather trot – always try to keep him moving at a steady pace) on your left side. Whether or not you intend showing him or training him for Obedience, there are always everyday occasions when you need to keep your right hand free. A Sheltie should never pull on the lead, so keep the lead fairly short but not too tight, encouraging the dog to move beside you without being so close that he will brush your leg. He will need to trot round you when you turn to the right, but to give way when you turn left. That is enough to learn for the time being – the refinements can come later.

## SOCIALISATION

As soon as your puppy is free from vaccination restrictions, he needs to learn how to behave among other dogs and people. After four months of age, this may become progressively more difficult, so it really is important to get the young dog out and about as soon as possible. Nowadays, more training clubs realise the importance of puppy socialisation, and there is an increasing number that hold 'puppy parties'

However, if your local club does not take puppies until six months of age, it is well worth joining your local breed club. Nearly every club (or its local branch) holds regular meetings covering all kinds of subjects, providing a useful balance between educational and social activities. Most will also put on a series of age-adjusted classes for puppies between the ages of three and twelve months. The conditions are very relaxed, offering a gentle way of teaching puppies to walk calmly on the lead, to be assessed by understanding strangers, to enjoy the company of other dogs, and to lie quietly while their owners juggle with the teacups and raffle-tickets!

For regular weekly classes, you will probably need to join a local Obedience Club. It would be a good idea to take advantage of the customary facility to sit in on one session (with or without your dog) to see whether it appears to be suitable. To begin with, you will be the pupil and the dog will be learning through you, so it would be a mistake to enrol under an instructor whose methods or personality you find unsympathetic. It would also be a good idea to watch a more advanced class at work.

## BASIC EXERCISES

The well-behaved companion Sheltie should be taught to respond to basic commands in order to fit in with everyday life. These will be taught at a training club, but it is worth making a start at home. Practice is essential, and you cannot expect your dog to restrict his learning to the training class situation, you must follow up with lessons at home.

The "Sit" is one of the easiest exercises to teach, and this is best taught when you are giving your puppy his dinner. As soon as the word is associated with the action, your puppy should respond without the enticement of sitting for his meal. If not, a firm pressure on the hindquarters, coupled with the command "Sit" will soon achieve the desired result.

Teaching the "Down" takes this exercise one step further. Tone of voice is all-important, and if you give the command in a low, firm voice, coupled with gentle pressure on the forequarters, plus a downward tug of the lead, your Sheltie will soon learn this exercise. We are lucky that Shelties are eager to please, and your puppy will be keen to do as you ask, as soon as he understands the request.

The "Stay" (as discussed previously) is a key command, and it is worth spending time to get your Sheltie absolutely steady in the "Stay". To begin with keep your puppy on a lead, and just move one step backwards, using a positive hand signal (palm held towards the dog) and give the command "Stay". If your puppy gets up and moves towards you, do not get cross. Just put your puppy back in the "Sit" and repeat the exercise. Gradually, you can increase the distance you leave your puppy, and then graduate to teaching the command off-lead. Patience is essential, and it is important that all training sessions are kept short and end on a good, positive note.

The Recall follows on from the "Stay", although you should separate these two

*ABOVE: Controlled precision work is required as the dog negotiates this obstacle.*

*BELOW: Just Dusty displays his skills over the hurdles – dogs find agility training both stimulating and exciting.*

*The Shetland Sheepdog is capable of competing at the highest level. Obedience Champion Carolelen Sno-Wonder is pictured competing at Crufts.*

exercises, as if you are not careful your puppy will get confused and will start to break the "Stay". For a recall, keep your puppy on the lead to start with. Command your puppy to "Sit", and back off to the end of the lead, giving the command "Wait" and using the appropriate hand signal (palm held towards the dog). When you have reached the end of the lead, wait a few moments before giving the command "Come" and giving a slight tug of the lead. This lesson can be stepped up gradually until you can leave your Sheltie sitting off the lead, walk away, turn and face, and then call your dog in.

## THE VERSATILE SHELTIE
## OBEDIENCE
Thousands of Sheltie owners all over the world get an enormous amount of interest from training their dogs, and certainly Shelties enjoy learning. For such demure little creatures they can be terrible show-offs!

As suggested previously, if you decide that you would like to join a weekly training class, do attend one session as a spectator to see whether you find the instructor(s) and the atmosphere congenial. For instance, you want to teach your Sheltie to tolerate big dogs, but you do not want the few delinquent giants, who are there to learn not to pounce playfully on small dogs, to use your dog as practice. Most breed clubs have an Obedience section, and so you may get the chance to train with other Sheltie owners, with an instructor who understands the Sheltie character.

The British Obedience structure is quite different from that in America, Canada and Australasia. These countries offer realistic conditions for Shelties to gain Companion Dog (CD), Companion Dog Excellent (CDX), Utility Dog (UD) and Utility Dog Excellent (UDX) qualifications in Obedience Trials. For instance, jumps are tailored to the size of the breed, but in Britain (where Working Trials originated to further the aims of police and army dogs) few concessions are made for smaller breeds. A dog that is just over fifteen inches must clear the same obstacles as a German Shepherd Dog. So although many Shelties have achieved CD Ex and UD Ex qualifications, most concentrate on Obedience competitions. Here, dogs work through graduated classes at graduated Obedience shows towards the ultimate title of Obedience Champion. The Sheltie has always been among the top three or four breeds in this discipline, and is certainly the most successful of the smaller breeds competing in Obedience.

## AGILITY
This is a fast-growing, fast-moving activity, which attracts enormous public interest. It demands initial Obedience training, as well as a high degree of physical fitness of both dog and owner. However, you must wait until your Sheltie is fully mature before enrolling on an agility course, as a growing dog should not be subjected to the physical stress that is involved in this activity. Even if you do not become a top competition winner, this sport is highly enjoyable for both dog and owner.

## FLY BALL
This is another very fast-moving attraction, and the sight of a number of teams of incredibly fast dogs running out and collecting the ball and then competing over hurdles in a hairs-breadth finish is nearly as exciting for the spectators as for the participants.

## THERAPY DOGS

This scheme has been evolved to encourage the use of pets as therapy (known as PAT dogs in the UK). After enrolment, the therapy dog owner is put in touch with officials of hospitals, schools, nursing and residential homes, who have expressed an interest in the project. The owner and dog will be expected to make regular visits (reliability is obviously important) to patients or residents, some of whom might otherwise receive few visitors. These visits have occasionally been of particular benefit to people who, after many years of loneliness, have become so withdrawn from human communication that a greeting to a dog may be the means of breaking a long silence.

The Sheltie is reassuringly quiet and gentle in his manner, and is therefore ideal for the purpose, and a large number are now enriching the lives of many, particularly the elderly and the infirm,

## HERDING

Although, as already suggested, the Sheltie's claim to be a herder is somewhat tenuous, they still have a trickle of working sheepdog blood in their veins, and the Breed Standard ensures that (with the obvious proviso of size) the breed's physical construction is compatible with the ability to work farm stock.

Organised Herding competitions are a relatively recent interest in America, where a number of Shelties have shown marked ability. This innovation has not yet spread to the UK, although Sheepdog Trials (for Border Collies) have always been a feature of country life.

Over the years, farmers have occasionally used show-bred Shetland Sheepdogs for working sheep on a practical level. However, the Sheltie cannot seriously be compared with the working Collie, which is probably a good thing from the pet owner's point of view. The true bred-in-the-bone worker has a deep *need* to work, and can be so frustrated by the lack of such a facility that it might be a difficult dog to live with.

## GOOD CITIZEN SCHEME

This scheme originated in the USA, and it has been adopted by other Kennel Clubs to encourage owners to train their dogs in elementary obedience. It consists of a series of basic exercises designed to ensure that the dogs tested can be relied upon to react in a calm and sensible way to a variety of everyday situations. It also ensures that the owners are qualified to handle, care for and be responsible for their pets. All breed clubs have details of the scheme and will provide the necessary training and testing.

# Chapter Five

# GROOMING AND BATHING

Hopefully, you would not have chosen the long-coated Shetland Sheepdog unless you were prepared to regard his beautiful coat as an essential part of his attraction. Luckily, whether you are grooming the show dog or the pet Sheltie, the process is a commonsense affair, well within the capability of any owner. It is simply a matter of keeping the dog clean and neat so that he is always comfortable and pleasing to the eye. Routine grooming takes, at most, half an hour once a week and it calls for no specialist skills – just a bit of practice. It would therefore be a waste of money to take a Sheltie to a professional grooming salon.

By eight weeks old the average Sheltie puppy will already have been persuaded to stand in a balanced posture on a table to be assessed by interested friends as well as his owner. Even if the pup is not intended for showing, it is a good idea to keep up this routine. A dog that is used to being handled by strangers in this way will be more amenable to the vet's attentions, as well as those of an owner needing to remove a tick or a tangled strand of bramble. In case of real emergency, the dog that is used to lying on its side for grooming is less likely to struggle during the treatment of an injury.

So even before there is need for serious grooming, every few days the young puppy should be placed carefully on a non-slip surface for a bit of fussing. On one occasion look at his teeth, the next time examine his feet, or maybe check the ears, so that your puppy gets used to these attentions. By the time the Sheltie is four months old, it is time to think of his permanent grooming requirements and to establish a weekly routine, preferably on the same day each week so that the occasion is not forgotten.

## GROOMING EQUIPMENT
If you buy equipment that is really suitable for this purpose, it will save you a lot of time and trouble. You will need:

BRUSH: Do not buy an ordinary 'dog-brush', no matter the type. For a Sheltie's coat you need a 'human' brush with fairly long bristles (these can be nylon) set in a rubber pad. Mason Pearson brushes (made in England) or Isinis brushes (made in France) are ideal, and they come in several sizes. The most suitable is the standard size, which is about 9ins (23cm) long including the handle, and 2.75ins (7cm) wide.

COMBS: A conventional steel comb, with teeth set fairly wide apart at one end and closer together at the other, will do for general purposes. They do vary a lot, so you

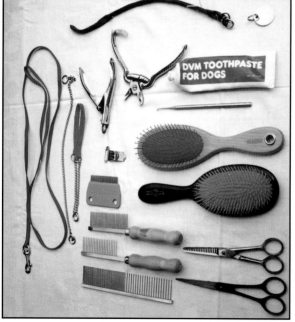

*ABOVE: The Sheltie coat needs regular grooming to ensure it does not become matted or tangled.*

*LEFT: Grooming kit needed by the Sheltie owner.*

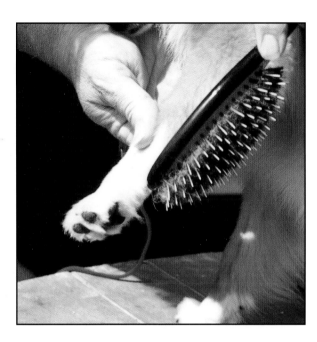

*When brushing your Sheltie, pay particular attention to the feathering.*

*The feet should be trimmed to neat oval shape, and the nails should be trimmed regularly.*

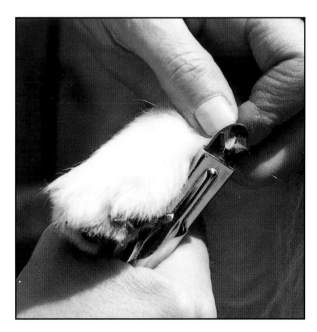

can only try them to find out which you prefer. A comb with very blunt, rounded teeth will not penetrate the coat, so you need one with fairly sharp teeth – but not so lethal as to draw blood when you pass a finger across them. A small tooth-comb will also be useful on occasions.

SCISSORS: A small, blunt-ended pair of scissors is needed for removing excess hair from the feet. A pair of thinning scissors is invaluable for trimming the soft hair from round the ears. The serrated type are the safest to use. You need about forty 'teeth' on one blade, and a conventional cutting edge on the other. Do not buy the type with about twenty teeth on both blades.

NAIL-CLIPPERS: A pair of guillotine type nail-clippers is the easiest to use.

## ROUTINE GROOMING
This is a simple procedure, but it does pay to be really thorough. First stand the dog on a table of convenient height, and get rid of any loose hair and/or dried mud by brushing the coat vigorously against the lie of the hair, and then brushing it back into place again. Pay special attention to the trousers and the underside of the tail. Then lay the dog on his side.

The idea is to groom right down to the skin by brushing out the coat in layers, a little at a time. Start with the long hair on the hind legs, immediately above the hock joint. Holding back the bulk of the coat with your left hand so as to create a 'parting', brush out the narrow fringe of hair in front of your hand, gradually moving your hand back so that more and more of the coat is brushed out right down to the skin. Every now and then you can use the comb to make sure that no tangles are left. Carry on brushing the chest and side, dealing gently with the fine, soft hair inside the flanks and under the arms. Deal with any urine stains by dusting in a little talcum powder and brushing it out again.

Turn the dog over and repeat the process on the other side. Then stand him up on the table and brush the back, all round the neck, the frill and the chest in just the same way, parting a little of the coat at a time and brushing it right down to the skin. Finish by giving a brisk brush upwards against the grain, then down in the natural lie of the coat before combing the dog gently all over to produce the neat, flowing outline.

## FEET
The saying "You are as young as your feet" certainly applies to dogs. Comfortable, neat feet will help to keep the Sheltie active and mobile into old age. Splayed feet, encouraged by over-long nails and pads spread by accumulations of muddy hair, will slow your Sheltie down until he is overweight, which will compound the problem.

If your Sheltie is given regular road-walking exercise, this will help to keep the nails short, but they may still need to be trimmed from time to time using nail-clippers. On the white foot the quick will be easy to detect, but dark nails are more difficult, so be cautious and cut off only the extreme tips, which will be pointed and slightly hooked. If you cut the quick it will cause the nail to bleed profusely. Check the dew claws (the 'thumbs') on the front legs. They will seldom need attention, but if neglected they may curl right round to penetrate the skin.

Next, with the blunt-ended scissors cut round the outline of the feet to produce the neat, oval shape. Then cut the hair on the underside of the feet so that it is level with the pads. Any clumps of muddy, gritty hair between the toes should be teased out with finger and thumb and then thinned or shortened with the scissors. There is no need to remove every hair from between the toes, as this could detract from the compact shape of the foot, and a little hair can give a certain amount of protection.

As each hind foot is completed, comb out the hair between the heel and the hock so that it stands out at right angles from the leg, and trim it with the serrated scissors, parallel with but not too close to the bone, before combing the hair back into place and neatening the heel with the scissors. When you return from a walk in the summer, always check for grass seeds which tend to travel up between the toes and which can penetrate the skin.

## TEETH
For some inexplicable reason, tartar collects far too readily on the teeth of some Shelties. If this is neglected, it can cause offensive breath and the loosening and premature loss of the teeth. Prevention is certainly better than cure, which can involve expensive treatment under anaesthetic.

The method of prevention the dog would choose is a nice meaty bone, but although I have allowed my dogs to have them over a great many years with only a couple of minor mishaps, I recommend them with reservations as they do present a slight hazard. There are many types of synthetic bone on the market now, and if your dog likes them (mine ignore them) they could be the ideal solution. Canine toothpaste can be obtained, complete with toothbrush, from your vet or from your local pet store.

Tartar first appears at the top of the canine teeth, and if it has not already made the gum too sore, it can be removed with the thumb-nail, the end of a nail-file or (preferably) with a dental scaler. If tartar has become a real problem, it must be removed under anaesthetic. Tragically, it has been known for a Sheltie to fail to survive this operation. There is a type of anaesthetic specifically recommended for elderly dogs or those suffering from kidney or liver problems, and this appears to suit Shelties. Most vets stock it and will use it on request.

## EARS
Breeders have worked very hard to improve ear carriage in the Shetland Sheepdog over the years, and if your Sheltie's ears tip naturally and grow short, neat hair, they will need little or no attention. However, many dogs tend to grow such long, straggly hair behind their ears that they look as though they are wearing bonnets. This hair needs to be shortened with the trimming scissors, and then thinned out with finger and thumb until the shape of the ear is revealed.

During teething, your puppy's ears may tend to prick. You may not be too concerned about this, particularly if you have no intentions of showing your Sheltie. But if you want to try to remedy the tendency, the best course of action is to consult your puppy's breeder. Breeders have different methods of coping with this problem, and the treatment depends on whether the dog is to be shown. In this case, any substance applied needs to be removed easily.

For the companion Sheltie, I think a good thick blob of antiseptic cream, applied under the actual tip of the ear, is the least fiddly method. To keep it in place you will need to sprinkle it with talcum powder. This will become absorbed only gradually

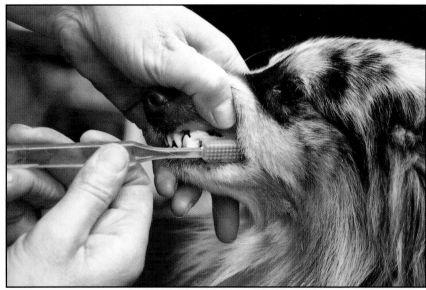

*Teeth should be brushed using a canine toothpaste.*

*If tartar accumulates on the teeth you need to use a tooth-scaler to remove it.*

*RIGHT: During teething your puppy's ears may prick, but the correct carriage is for the ear to tip.*

*BELOW: The Sheltie should be thoroughly groomed before bathing.*

and the grease will continually seep through, so you must keep applying talcum powder, flattening the blob with your thumb as it dries. Then just leave it to wear out as the hair grows. This growing out or wearing away process may take weeks rather than days. By this time the ear carriage may be corrected. Otherwise it means starting again.

American breeders use much more sophisticated methods of correcting ear carriage. Sometimes remedial action will be taken as a matter of routine, without waiting to see whether correction is required. As well as dealing with the actual 'drop' of the ear, the angle at which the ear is carried may be corrected or anticipated by bracing the ears of a young puppy and drawing them together more closely on top of the skull  Such methods can be extremely effective, but considerable dexterity is needed in applying them and the inexperienced owner will require 'hands on' tuition before acquiring the necessary skill.

Fortunately, so much progress has been made in the direction of breeding out these problems that the naturally well-carried ear is very much the rule rather than the exception. For many breeders, the troublesome ear is just an occasional phenomenon.

## BATHING

Provided your Sheltie is groomed weekly, he will not need frequent bathing. For pet and show dog alike, a bath is advisable to remove the last vestiges of coat towards the end of moulting, and to ensure that the skin is clean and free from dandruff before the new hair grows in.

Show dogs can also be bathed when the coat is losing its brightness and sheen. Dry shampoo is seldom a good idea, as it is likely to make the coat look and feel tacky, and it is uncomfortable for the dog. Show dogs must also have their white markings meticulously washed immediately before every show.

The family bath is not the best place for this job, not necessarily for hygienic reasons (a bath is easily cleaned), but because you cannot bath a dog at ground level – all that stretching and bending is agony for your back! A large sink in a utility room is ideal. Free-standing dog baths that do not require plumbing are obtainable, but they constitute a considerable investment.

Before bathing, your Sheltie must be groomed thoroughly, otherwise any loose hair will become lumpy and matted, taking hours to dry and comb out. This is particularly important when the dog is moulting. Shelties are usually very cooperative at bathtime, but it is as well to equip yourself with a waterproof apron before running the luke-warm water and gathering all the essentials together.

You will need shampoo (insecticidal, if necessary) suitably decanted and diluted in a plastic bottle, a tablet of soap, a plastic jug for rinsing and a pile of clean, warm towels. Old tea-towels are worth saving as they absorb a surprising amount of water during the initial squeezing out process.

Encourage your dog to sit while you do your best to wet him all over – not an easy task as the Sheltie's coat is designed to be water-repellent. First wash the legs and feet with the solid soap, which is easily rubbed into the hair and between the toes. Then, starting at the rear end, not forgetting the tail, work plenty of shampoo into the coat as far as the shoulders. Do not neglect the underneath and inside the thighs. Rinse this off and apply more shampoo which will lather more easily. Then tackle the neck and chest, again shampooing twice. Do not touch the head or ears.

Using fresh luke-warm water, rinse thoroughly at least twice. Remove the dog from the water and squeeze the worst of the wet out before using the towels.

When the dog is partially dry, complete the process with an electric hair-dryer. Provided you do not startle your dog by switching straight to highest speed, most dogs soon learn to tolerate the dryer – some positively enjoy it. When the dog is nearly dry, it is useful to get him to lie on his side so that you can groom him as usual, continuing to use the dryer as you brush and comb. Before releasing your Sheltie to lie in his favourite warm corner, make sure he is quite dry, or his coat will wave where he has been lying, and it is extraordinary how difficult it is to eliminate such a kink from the coat.

*ABOVE: The judge goes over each dog individually assessing overall construction.*

*LEFT: The Sheltie must be taught to stand in show stance in order to show himself to advantage.*

# Chapter Six

# SHOWING THE SHELTIE

If dog breeding is an obsessive and expensive hobby, then dog showing is a compulsive and financially ruinous one! However, it is very natural that a proud owner, having bought or bred a promising puppy, will soon become interested in assessing him against his contemporaries. It is quite impossible to explain the lure of all the early rising, the constant long-distance travelling, and the running battles with extremes of weather. It is also difficult to maintain the endless cash-flow (all in one direction, as there is no prize-money). But it is a strange fact that showing rapidly becomes a maddening, eccentric, but exhilarating way of life.

*Once you have been bitten by the show-going bug, there is no turning back!*

## THE SHOW SCENE
### BRITAIN
Britain has a complicated show system. Some events are very informal in character, but all are licensed by the Kennel Club. Primary, Sanction and Limited shows all have a restricted scope in accordance with a dog's previous wins. They exclude Challenge Certificate winners and Champions from competition.

Open shows cater for all dogs including Champions, but they do not offer qualifications towards the title of Champion. Championship shows, whether all-breed or single breed events, offer Challenge Certificates. To attain the title of Champion a dog must win a minimum of three Challenge Certificates under three different judges.

### UNITED STATES
Matches are the most informal of the American shows and entries are made on the morning of the show. They are often used as a training ground for people who are aspiring to judge at Championship show level. Championship shows can be all breed, Group or breed Specialty Shows. Points are awarded towards the Championship title by a judge who is approved by the American Kennel Club.

A total of fifteen points under three different judges must be gained for a dog to become a Champion, including two 'majors' under separate judges (3, 4, or 5 point wins). The size of the major is decided by the number of dogs entered at a show. The scale of Championship points is decided by the American Kennel Club, and this is calculated on the average number of Shetland Sheepdogs shown in various regions of the USA.

Specialties are held annually or bi-annually by the club concerned, usually attracting large entries. Again, Championship points are awarded. The judge is normally someone held in high esteem by breeders and exhibitors, and sometimes an overseas judge receives an invitation to officiate.

### PREPARING YOUR DOG
Before you enter your dog at a show, it is advisable to go along as a spectator, and then you will learn something of the procedure and what is required before you are actually competing.

The grooming procedure will be similar to the routine you have been following for months. The dogs may or may not have been bathed before the show, but their white markings will certainly have been thoroughly washed, ears neatened and feet trimmed the evening before the event.

The only preparation to be seen at a British show nowadays is routine brushing and combing with, possibly, a light spraying with water to 'lift' the coat. No other aids are permitted. However, it is always interesting to watch dogs being skilfully groomed, and provided you do not interrupt last-minute preparation, most exhibitors will be glad to show you, for instance, how a dog's ears have been neatened, and will tell you where to obtain the necessary tools. The source will almost certainly be a big Championship show, where a treasurehouse of trade stands will supply anything from a collar to a kennel.

### IN THE SHOW RING
All show entries are entered in a catalogue, so you can identify the dogs in the ring

and their parentage. In each class (which are divided according to age, sex, and, in the UK, previous wins) all the dogs will be moved round the ring in an anti-clockwise direction, in a brisk and orderly fashion before each exhibit in turn is examined on the table. As each dog is removed from the table to demonstrate its movement, the next will immediately take its place so that the handler will have it posed to advantage when the judge is ready to look at it. While maintaining a position to be able to control the dog if necessary, the exhibitor must take care not to impede the judge.

Each dog will be moved in the judge's preferred pattern, and it is the responsibility of exhibitors to have observed this so that there is no delay in carrying out the required procedure. Show training classes will have taught you how to move in a triangle, making the most of the available space and turning each corner as smoothly as possible so as not to check or jerk your dog. Remember that the dog will always be on the inside as you turn. If you are asked to move across the ring in a straight line, this may be to show your dog's movement both coming and going. If, however, you notice that the judge has moved to the side of the ring, it will be to assess the gait in profile. In this case you will have to change the lead smoothly from one hand to the other at one end of the ring, so that the dog will always be between you and the judge. Incidentally, if strips of matting are provided, this will be for the benefit of the dogs, not the handlers. Sadly, provided we do not fall flat on our faces, nobody cares much whether we pin-in or toe-out!

By the time the last dog has been moved, all the others will be posed ready for the judge's final attention. This also gives the onlooker a good chance to evaluate the dogs, and then to compare mental placings with the judge's final placings.

## WHAT THE JUDGE IS LOOKING FOR
The judge's task is to assess all the dogs that are entered against the Breed Standard. This is the blueprint of the breed, originally drawn up by breed specialists, and published by the national Kennel Cub. The Breed Standard may vary slightly from country to country, but this is in detail only.

Briefly, the judge will hope to see a small, abundantly-coated working dog which should be strong and active, lithe and graceful, but never coarse or cloddy. The outline will be symmetrical so that no part appears to be out of proportion to the whole. The refined, smoothly moulded, wedge-shaped head will be carried proudly on a reachy, well-arched neck, which will flow smoothly into a graceful topline completed by a long, low-set, low-carried tail. The eyes will be of medium size, almond-shaped and obliquely set; together with the semi-erect, responsive ears, they will give a sweet, alert, gentle expression.

The body will be slightly longer from the point of the shoulder to the bottom of the croup. The chest should reach the elbows. The forelegs should be straight with strong, but not over-heavy bone. The feet must be neatly oval in shape with tightly arched, well-padded toes. The hindquarters should be well-muscled and well-angulated. For details of the function and interplay of the fore and hindquarters which produce the correct lithe, smooth, graceful movement, you must study the Breed Standard carefully.

An American judge might place the dogs in a different order from his British counterpart as he would be working from a Standard which, though apparently almost identical in essential requirements, varies in seemingly minor details. The

*Championship shows in Britain are benched, but that is not the case in the United States.*

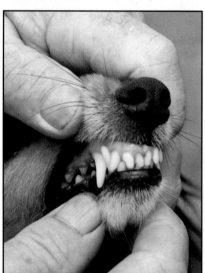

*The mouth will be examined to check for the correct scissor bite.*

*You may wish to tidy up your Sheltie by trimming the featherings.*

*Ch. Jack Point of Janetstown: The British judge is looking for an abundantly-coated working dog which should be graceful in outline with a fine head and a sweet expression.*

*Anne Roslin-Williams.*

*Beltane Chip Off The Old Block: The American judge is looking for a leaner skull combined with a slightly heavier muzzle than the British counterpart, and for slightly heavier bone.*

judge would be looking for a differently wedged shape when assessing the head, probably preferring a proportionately leaner skull combined with a slightly heavier muzzle. The extra emphasis placed on a strong underjaw would also indicate a preference for a more blunt wedge when the head is viewed from the side.

The American Standard calls only for a 'somewhat' oblique eye placement and ears that are carried three-fourths erect, a combination which might result in a slightly different expression. The American Sheltie is allowed a slightly more jaunty tail carriage when alert. This, combined with the fact that the tail is not specifically required to be low-set, could explain why to the British judge, the rear of an American Sheltie sometimes seems a little squared-off.

Finally, there is the question of size, again apparently infinitesimal in fact, but more noticeable in effect. The ideal height for a British Sheltie dog is 14.5ins (37cm), and 14ins (35.5cm) for a bitch. One inch above or below these heights is considered 'highly undesirable' in Kennel Club parlance. The American Standard is less specific, giving an overall size range of 13-16ins with no differentiation between the sexes, but there is a disqualification for any individual measuring over or under these shoulder heights. The problem here is made more by nature than by man, for it is usually the case that, where small animal species are concerned, nature will tend to favour the upper limit, which gradually becomes the norm.

# Chapter Seven

# BREEDING SHELTIES

## TO BREED OR NOT TO BREED?

Dog breeding is an utterly absorbing hobby, but it is also costly and potentially worrying. It often has legal or environmental implications, so it is advisable to consider the following practical considerations.

1. It is *not* necessary to breed one litter from a bitch 'for the sake of her health'.
2. World-wide, many authorities (especially welfare organisations drawn into the problems of canine over-population) are in favour of neutering both dogs and bitches. In some places, neutered animals are subject to lower licensing rates.
3. To breed from a bitch which has not been registered is not only pointless, but it could also lead to serious problems when attempting to sell the progeny.
4. The fact must be faced that within the foreseeable future it could become increasingly difficult to find suitable homes for puppies. To be faced with the possibility of having apparently unwanted dogs on which you have spent so much time and effort, so much cash and such affection could be physically exhausting, financially crippling and emotionally draining.
5. Shelties usually have strong constitutions and are free from any constructional abnormalities, and they are generally considered to be particularly easy whelpers. However, it has to be remembered that where breeding is concerned, worries and risks are seldom too far away and 'easy' can be a comparative term!

## THE BROOD BITCH

If, after weighing up the pros and cons, you are still keen to breed a litter, the next step is to contact your bitch's breeder, who will confirm that it is advisable to go ahead, and may also help to choose a suitable stud dog. The male should, of course, be free from hereditary diseases; his breeding should be compatible with that of the bitch, he should not duplicate any obvious fault she may have, but he should also have some positive virtues to offer. Simple!

It is best not to breed from a Sheltie bitch before she is about eighteen months old, by which time her second season will probably be due. It is advisable to book the stud service well in advance. The majority of bitches come into season in January and February, and so dogs are likely to be very busy then and may not be able to oblige a last-minute date. This is a good time to mate a bitch as it means a Spring litter. The first indication that the bitch is about to come in season is that she may urinate more frequently than usual. Keep a close eye on her, watching for a slightly enlarged vulva with the slightest suspicion of a creamy discharge. This will

*The stud dog must be sound in construction and temperament and free from any hereditary problems.*

ABOVE:
The brood bitch should be a typical example of the breed, and her breeding should tie in with the stud dog.

LEFT: The proof of good breeding (pictured left to right): Ch. Forestland Tassel, Forestland Royal Bloom and Ch. Forestland Farmers Boy.

rapidly turn red and become much more copious. For the first week or more the vulva will become much bigger and very hard and red. By about the twelfth day the vulva, still quite enlarged, will be much softer and more lax. The discharge may begin to lessen and will be paler in colour.

If you touch the bitch around her rear she may give you a scandalized look and sit down hurriedly, in which case she is not quite ready. When she responds by gazing thoughtfully into the distance, while raising her tail so that it is rigid at the root but switched round sideways, things look very hopeful. Do not leap into the car immediately, but telephone the dog's owner who will probably give you another tip or two, to prevent a premature trip. Before you start on your journey, let the bitch into the garden to relieve herself. Then brush her petticoats to ensure they are not soiled by excreta (but do not clean up the discharge) and off you go, arriving as punctually as possible.

## THE MATING

The stud dog owner will take control of the mating, but your help and cooperation will probably be appreciated, and your bitch will be reassured by your presence. You will doubtless be asked to sit facing the bitch with one hand tucked into each side of her collar, your thumbs resting firmly against the base of her ears so that, without throttling her, you could prevent her from whipping round suddenly. This is only a precaution as the whole affair may be conducted without the slightest drama. However, even if initially flirtatious, maiden bitches can be capricious, and you need to prevent any sudden movements at your end. The dog's owner will be looking after the rear. The bitch may cry out as the dog penetrates, but she is more likely to become apprehensive and fidgety as the tie begins to take effect. This occurs when the dog's penis swells and is held in the vulva by the bitch's contracting muscles. After a few seconds she will probably settle down. Soon the dog can be turned and everybody can relax, while remaining watchful.

Most dogs tie for ten to twenty minutes. If things go on for very much longer than half-an-hour both parties get a bit bored and one or the other may try to take evasive action by pulling away or even trying to roll over on to the floor. This must, of course, be prevented. Eventually all will terminate naturally. It is a good idea to return the bitch immediately to the car to rest while you complete the formalities. Do not forget to pick up the necessary Kennel Club form together with the dog's pedigree. You will be expected to pay for the service right away, but should the bitch 'miss' you will probably be offered a repeat mating at her next season, free of charge. After mating, the bitch must be kept right away from other dogs until her season is completely finished.

## WATCHING AND WAITING

A bitch's normal gestation period is sixty-three days, but Shelties frequently whelp a couple of days early. Some anticipate the event by four or five days without ill effect. There is much less tendency for them to go over sixty-three days, which is just as well for our nerves!

The first sign that a bitch is in whelp may be noticed as early as three weeks when her teats will become pinker and more prominent. At three weeks it is also possible for a vet to confirm the pregnancy by palpation. A bit later, an ultrasound scanner can usually detect puppies and their movements, but unless there is an important reason for wishing to confirm pregnancy, there is little point in spending a lot of money doing this.

During pregnancy, the bitch should be kept to her normal feeding and exercise routine. While exercising, you may notice a thick, sticky, almost colourless discharge – a very good omen which will persist right up to the time the bitch whelps. By five weeks there should be a slight thickening of the waist, which is an indication that you can start, very gradually, to increase the bitch's diet. The increase should be in protein (in the shape of good-quality raw meat) rather than in bulk-food. Toward the end of the pregnancy, your bitch should be getting a pound of meat a day and as much milk as she wants, provided you know she can tolerate it – not all Shelties can, and the last thing you need to do is to upset her digestion. The increase in quantity should be gradual, and the meals should be divided into three or four smallish meals rather than over-burdening the stomach with large meals. Sufficient biscuit should be added to balance the meal, but it should not be increased at the same rate as the protein.

If your bitch cannot tolerate milk, a calcium supplement can be added to her food in whichever form seems appropriate. If the powdered type discourages her from cleaning the dish, tablets are available, which you will know she has swallowed. If in doubt, the vet will provide you with a suitable supplement. Do not give two different supplements, and do not increase the recommended dosage.

During the final couple of weeks of pregnancy, exercise should be more sedate, and your bitch should be discouraged from jumping on and off furniture or in and out of the car.

## PREPARATIONS FOR WHELPING

Before, during and after whelping, the bitch (and subsequently the puppies) will need constant supervision, so the first consideration is deciding where the bitch is to whelp. Many people opt for the kitchen. If the family is small and the kitchen large, this is often a convenient arrangement. I, personally, prefer the peace and quiet of my bedroom. Wash-basin, medicine cupboard, heating and drying facilities are to hand, and nobody else need be disturbed. So once the bitch and I have come to an agreement that she is now too cumbersome to leap on my bed, we can settle down comfortably for as long as it takes.

If you plan to breed more than one litter it is worth buying a custom-made whelping box, but if this is to be a one-time event, a wooden box about 30ins (76cms) by 20ins (50cms), and 22ins (56cms) in height, would make a generous home for an average Sheltie litter. A strip of wood will have to be fixed across the bottom of the box to retain the bedding and the puppies, but when they are up and about, this barrier can be removed to allow them free access and exit. A hinged or removable lid is useful. If the box is a bit rough it can be lined with thick, deeply corrugated cardboard, which will provide excellent insulation. The floor of the box should also be lined with newspaper.

Once the bitch knows where the whelping box is located, she may take herself off to it at intervals to scratch tentatively at the bedding. You will be touched to notice how carefully, even at this early stage, she will step in and out of the box. Instinct is taking over already. By late pregnancy all the hair on her abdomen will have dropped out. This area should be carefully washed, and a fair amount of hair should be cut from her rear and from underneath her tail, for this is the somewhat

*LEFT: Shetland Sheepdog puppies pictured just one hour after birth.*

*BELOW: The brood bitch nurses her litter, four days after birth.*

ABOVE: The puppies should be kept clean and warm – their eyes will open when they are about ten days old.

RIGHT: By five weeks of age the puppies are eating solid food and becoming increasingly independent.

unattractive but warm and cosy area where puppies tend to congregate between meals. It is all too easy for one of them to get caught in the long hair, which gets very messy during and after whelping. A pup could strangle itself, or could be left swinging, to be knocked against the base-board of the box if the bitch gets out too quickly. Ridiculous as this sounds, it is a good idea to count heads whenever the bitch leaves the box, just in case a puppy is about to make an unscheduled trip into the garden hitched up in mother's petticoats.

## SIGNS OF IMMINENT WHELPING

For about a week before the event you will have felt the puppies' movements, which may even be visible when the bitch is lying quietly. After a few false alarms – when you hear her scratching up her bed quite vigorously – the evening will come when she will refuse her supper. The very greedy bitch may eat her meal, but she will inevitably bring it up again just before or during whelping. This is quite normal. Almost certainly her temperature will have dropped noticeably. She will probably whelp in the early hours of the following morning. By now you should have at hand:

A small pair of scissors (to be sterilized before use).
A roll of paper towelling or a box of large 3-ply tissues.
A few old towels.
A cardboard box, just big enough to contain a hot-water bottle or heating pad.
A couple of old jumpers to use as bedding in the cardboard box.
A flannelette sheet.
A small heater to top up the temperature or warm up a puppy.
A piece of synthetic fleece cut to fit the box exactly.
A large bin-bag for discarded newspaper etc.

Last minute behaviour varies, but the average bitch will become very restless and vaguely anxious. She may be quite excitable, jumping up and trying to get on your lap. Give her a quietly reassuring word, but do not make too much of a fuss. Eventually she will go back to her bed and start scratching and tearing up the paper quite feverishly, ripping it with her teeth and panting. She will appear to settle down for a while only to start the performance all over again. This can go on for hours, and it is only when you see the first real straining movement that you need look at your watch to time events. You should check that the room temperature is at least 21 degrees Centigrade (70 degrees Fahrenheit). If not, there is still time to raise it with the aid of the heater.

## WHELPING

As the straining becomes more obvious and more frequent, the bitch may lie, squat or stand and as she arches her back in a contraction, she may cry out or grunt. You may or may not notice the arrival of a small, dark water-bag, but you will certainly notice the green-stained wet patch it will leave on the paper when it bursts.

The first puppy should arrive soon (within half an hour or so). The pup will be encased in its protective membrane, and it will still be attached to the placenta which will be evacuated with it. The bitch should immediately tear away the membrane before chewing off the cord, and then (most probably) eating the afterbirth. Remember to check that an afterbirth arrives with or soon after the puppy – you will need to know if one or more has been retained. The bitch will lick the pup very thoroughly, pushing it around until it squeaks in protest before crawling off to a teat and, hopefully, starting to feed while the bitch prepares to cope with the next arrival.

Try to insert some clean, dry paper into the box as each puppy arrives or the others will get wet again. Some time during the procedure you will probably be able to remove each puppy in turn to dry it, check its sex and see that all is well. If all goes really smoothly, the pups will arrive at twenty to fifty minute intervals, though the timing is very erratic and the bigger the litter, the faster the puppies may arrive.

This is copybook scenario, and, of course, there are many variations. Sometimes a maiden bitch will ignore the first puppy which, if left unattended for too long, will become chilled, and unless the enclosing membrane is cleared away it will suffocate and die. In such a case, quickly remove the membrane from the head, clearing away any liquid or mucus from mouth and nose with a tissue. If the pup does not move or cry out, hook your finger into its mouth to make sure its tongue has not rolled back to obstruct the airway. It will probably gasp, cry out or even grasp your finger with astonishing strength. This one will probably be quite alright, so offer it back to the bitch.

If she still does not catch on, remove the rest of the membrane, pinch the cord firmly a couple of inches from the puppy's navel, and, pulling away from the placenta rather than the puppy, tear it apart between your thumbs and forefingers. This is the way the bitch would do it and the gradual shredding will cause less bleeding than a cut with scissors. However, if you have had time to sterilize your scissors, you can use them instead. It is unlikely nowadays that any puppy will have a dewclaw on a hind leg, but if this should occur make a mental note that it must be removed by the vet within three or four days.

When all the puppies have arrived, the bitch will relax and settle down peacefully with her family. Offer her a drink of warm milk, or cool water if she prefers. Do not leave the dish in the bed, however, as she is sure to upset it deliberately and quite instinctively. Next, try to persuade your bitch to go out and relieve herself so that you can remove all the soiled paper from the bed, replacing it with some sheets of newspaper covered by the fleece bedding.

## THE NURSING BITCH AND PUPPIES
When the bitch returns, make sure all the puppies are feeding strongly, as this first milk contains the colostrum which is not only particularly nutritious, but also contains the antibodies which will protect the puppies from infection between birth and the time for vaccination. If one pup seems to be having problems with feeding you must try to help. This can be done by holding the pup at a teat, making sure that it is on top of his tongue, and expressing a little milk into his mouth. It sounds easy, but it takes a lot of patience and a tiny puppy can be extraordinarily stubborn. Hold him in place until you think he has had a good meal, or he will be pushed away by a stronger puppy.

During the first night (what is left of it!) the pups may be a bit squeaky and complaining; they have to adjust themselves to a totally new existence. But within twelve hours or so they will have settled down, and for the next couple of weeks you can look forward to a lovely peaceful time just watching them grow bigger and more beautiful by the day. Their mother will do all the work – washing, feeding and

*Good rearing is the key to a bright, alert, healthy puppy.*

*A nice, evenly-matched litter ready to explore the outside world.*

*A play-pen is ideal for rearing puppies, giving them the opportunity to enjoy the fresh air while still being safe and secure.*

clearing up. Make the most of this restful lull – your turn will come all too soon!

A Sheltie bitch is likely to have twice as many teats as she has puppies, and since the pups will be determined to use the most comfortable convenient ones in the shelter of her flanks, the smaller ones nearer her front legs will be unused. It is little use trying to make them use all the teats in turn; the effort will only make you frustrated and is bound to end in defeat. This means that the small front teats may get very hard within three or four days, in which case it is wise to apply hot fomentations to them several times a day for the next couple of days. Provided they are not stimulated, the milk will ebb away from these particular teats and all will be well. Neglect of this chore, however, could result in mastitis – an infection in the mammary glands. By the time they are a week old the puppies' toenails will have become very sharp, and unless you keep them trimmed regularly the bitch will be very painfully scratched. All you need to do is trim off the little hooked portion of the nail with a small pair of scissors, taking care to avoid the quick, which is fairly easily seen at this age. This job will have to be repeated every few days until the puppies are completely weaned. By about twelve days the puppies' eyes will start to open, very gradually and not necessarily all at the same time. They will immediately become personalities, starting to bumble around and rough one another up. Before they are three weeks old, they will be able to scramble up to the edge of the whelping box, and so it is time to get the barricades up before there is any risk of an accident occurring. It is probably worth investing in a puppy-pen, consisting of wire mesh panels which can be hinged together to make variable shapes and sizes. It is easier to fix one panel to the front edge of each side of the box so that to begin with you have a little 'run' the same width as the box, but twice as long.

As the puppies grow, you can enlarge the run to whatever shape and size is convenient. It must be placed on a piece of vinyl of appropriate size (if the room is not already vinyl floored) and covered by a couple of thicknesses of paper. After various heart-stopping experiences, I prefer to protect the lower part of the panels with very fine chicken-wire or plastic mesh to discourage heads or legs from poking through. The pens can be used indoors or outside for every conceivable purpose and will last for years. At this early stage, however, one of the panels must be replaced by a lower barricade so that the bitch can jump in and out easily.

## POST-WHELPING PROBLEMS

Hopefully, all will go smoothly, and your bitch will soon recover her health and strength  after whelping. However, there are a couple of conditions which are rare but potentially fatal, and so it is advisable to know the signs so that you are in a position to respond swiftly if the situation arises.

## METRITIS

This condition is an inflammation of the womb, and it can occur within twenty-four to forty-eight hours after whelping. The bitch will refuse food and will have a very high temperature. She will seem very lethargic and may be unsteady on her feet. There will be a very profuse, brownish, extremely foul-smelling discharge. She is obviously very ill indeed, and unless treatment is immediately forthcoming she may become comatose and die. Get her to the vet without delay, as the administration of an expellant drug and antibiotics will usually ensure rapid recovery. Among the most likely causes are the retention of a placenta or of a dead puppy.

## ECLAMPSIA

Also known as 'milk fever', this condition may occur a couple of weeks after whelping. It is caused by a sudden draining of calcium from the system as a result of feeding the puppies. The bitch may appear nervous and unsettled, and she may suffer muscular spasms, moving stiffly or going into an apparent fit. Again, immediate veterinary treatment (calcium injection) is vital and usually produces immediate recovery.

## WEANING

This process can start at about three weeks. I prefer to begin with a taste of meat. You will use so little in terms of quantity, it is worth buying the best beef steak, and this can be processed in the food-mixer to a paste-like consistency. The puppies will suck a little from a finger to begin with. The processed meat can be placed in varying sized blobs on to a sheet of waxed paper and stored in the freezer or, when frozen, it can be transferred to plastic bags each containing enough meat servings for the whole litter for a day.

No matter what the age of the puppies, meat meals are always fed individually. These can be increased gradually until at eight weeks each pup is getting two meals of about an ounce of meat, plus a little soaked wholemeal puppy-meal, increasing from a teaspoonful at four weeks to a dessertspoonful at eight weeks.

The first milk meal is given a day or two after the first meat meal. Goat's milk, once considered indispensable for rearing puppies, because it approximates much more closely to bitch's milk, disappeared for years from the market. Happily, it is now back and can be bought fresh or frozen. If this is not available locally, canned evaporated milk made up with warm water to twice the strength recommended for babies (puppies grow a lot faster than babies) can be given instead. A baby cereal can be added to this to produce a creamy consistency.

Each puppy, in turn, must be taught to lap this from a small, shallow bowl. They will all start by nose-diving into the bowl and producing spectacular bubbles, but as soon as they are lapping properly, a teaspoonful of honey can be added to the bowl of milk and cereal, and the puppies can be fed communally. By five weeks the baby cereal can be replaced by a wheat cereal, which seems to contain just the right amount of roughage to prevent diarrhoea. Experience will show you how much to use per feed, and this will change as the puppies grow.

So now the pups will be getting four meals a day, two meat-based, two milk-based, fed alternately. The meat will still be fed individually, the milk feed will be fed communally. A week or so before the pups are due to go to their new homes, one or two canned meat meals may be given in place of the raw meat, just to give the puppies a little variety so that they will not be upset by any changes introduced once they are out of your tender care.

## WORMING

It is now customary to worm young puppies at an earlier age and more frequently than was formerly the case. Since it can be extremely dangerous to over-dose young puppies, it is advisable to get a suitable treatment from the vet, and you must adhere very closely to the instructions regarding the strength and timing of dosing.

*It will not be long before your puppies have become fully independent from their mother and will be ready to go to new homes.*

*It is a sad moment when the time for parting comes, but you have the satisfaction of knowing that you have given your puppies the best possible start in life.*

# Chapter Eight

# HEALTH CARE

Shelties are strong, healthy dogs who generally live on well into their teens, without running up too many bills at the vet. Of course, they are subject to the most common canine ills, but are particularly prone to only a few. One of their weaknesses is a tendency to collect tartar on their teeth (See Chapter 5: Grooming and Bathing). Older dogs are sometimes inclined to kidney trouble. If this is suspected, the vet should be consulted right away, as apart from any specific treatment, some dietary adjustment may be indicated. The important thing is to notice the very first sign, which will generally be a tendency to drink more than usual.

When a Sheltie has come to the end of the road, the truly caring owner will not delay the inevitable in the hope that the dog will die peacefully in his own bed, thus saving you the heartache of making the final decision. This 'easy' solution seldom happens, and when it does, it may not be quite as you had expected. It will still be a shock. You will wonder whether he suffered and will reproach yourself because he was alone. It is then that you realise that it might have been kinder to take him to the vet for what the dog would consider just another inoculation. You would have been there to reassure him as usual, and afterwards you would understand how privileged we are to be able to give our dogs such a kindly end.

## VACCINATION
It is impossible to be absolutely specific about this important subject owing to the constant progress of science against disease. At the present time, immunization against distemper, hepatitis, leptospirosis and parvovirus is effected by a course of vaccinations (two or three according to the vaccine used). The first is usually given not earlier than eight weeks of age, and the final one not earlier than twelve weeks – but there are variations. The timing must be carefully regulated as otherwise the natural (but temporary) immunization passed to the puppy from its mother may neutralize the effect of the vaccine. Such discrepancies could account for the very rare so-called 'breakdowns' or adverse reactions which have occasionally been reported.

Only those who remember the days when the term 'over distemper' was an adult dog's most valid selling point, can fully appreciate today's freedom from such scourges. Time has shown that the many claims regarding prevention or cure of these diseases have been doomed to failure. Only one ('natural feeding') has retained some small semblance of credibility. Unfortunately, anybody who still places faith in this theory is sitting on a time-bomb, the explosion of which is delayed only by everybody else's adherence to the vaccination routine. Of course, ideal feeding plays an important part in maintaining a dog's health and stamina. But it is only today's very wide vaccination cover that prevents the build-up of viral epidemics.

BOOSTERS: The maintenance of a dog's life-long resistance to distemper etc. by adherence to a realistic 'booster' programme is highly advisable. It is recommended that a dog recieves a booster injection every twelve months. Before accepting a dog for boarding, nearly all kennels require proof that a dog's vaccination programme is up-to-date. So it is important to keep the original document in a safe place and to produce it for updating every time a dog visits the vet for boosting.

## KENNEL COUGH

This extremely contagious condition is not (as might be assumed) confined to breeding or boarding kennels. It may be contracted in any situation where numbers of dogs are gathered together – at shows, training classes, or even at the vet's surgery, should any client be inconsiderate enough to ignore the notice often displayed on the door of the premises. This requests the owner of a coughing dog to leave it outside in the car where it can be examined.

In normal circumstances, kennel cough is not lethal and an otherwise fit dog usually makes a complete recovery, but in kennels it can hang around for quite a time as one dog passes it on to its fellows. It can have distressing effects on young puppies or elderly dogs who may find it very difficult to shake off.

Unfortunately, kennel cough is a composite disease consisting of a number of different viruses, so vaccination can sometimes be regarded as an alleviation rather than as a certain preventative or cure. However, research continues and it is probably only a matter of time before a fully comprehensive vaccine becomes available. In the meantime, most boarding kennels will require proof of immunization against kennel cough as well as distemper and other commmunicable diseases.

## SKIN PARASITES

It might be assumed that, being long-coated dogs, Shelties are susceptible to skin trouble but fortunately this is not so. The only drawback posed by their long coats is that some conditions might go undetected for longer than would otherwise be the case. Regular grooming will ensure that this problem does not arise.

As with humans, a mild rash can mean anything or nothing (some dogs can be allergic to the young, new growth of nettles), but no skin trouble should be ignored. If it does not respond to careful cleansing followed by an application of antiseptic powder or lotion (whichever seems appropriate), the dog should be referred to the vet for diagnosis, possibly by laboratory analysis aided by skin-scrapings. Inadequately treated skin trouble can drag on for months, and apart from the frustration to the owner, such delay does nothing for the condition of a Sheltie's coat.

## FLEAS

Occasional infestation may result from contact with affected dogs or from rabbits or hedgehogs, but fleas should not be considered to be the inevitable companions of the well-kept dog! Signs of infestation should be noticed during routine grooming (or

*The long-coated Sheltie needs regular grooming to avoid problems with skin parasites.*

*The inoculation programme starts in puppyhood, and annual boosters must be given throughout your dog's life.*

from the dog's scratching) when either fleas or their dirts (tiny black, gritty particles) can be seen. Many remedies are available, but the vet will be able to supply the most suitable spray, powder or wash, as well as detailed instructions for application.

This is important as such remedies are necessarily pretty strong, and it is most important to use them with care. Any such application should be kept well away from the eyes and should not be inhaled. Do not forget that any powder applied to the Sheltie coat will be quite difficult to remove, so application should not be overdone and removal should be thorough.

## LICE
These tiny greyish blood-sucking insects are more difficult to detect and not as easy to eradicate as fleas. The vet should be consulted.

## TICKS
These blood-sucking parasites can be the unwelcome result of a lovely walk across sheep populated moorland. By the time they are noticed they will probably be already embedded in the skin. Seen first as tiny brownish insects, they will eventually become engorged to much bigger, tubular, greyish objects, ready, with any luck to drop to the ground. If still embedded, (often around the dog's head or neck) the tick can be carefully removed by grasping it firmly with a good pair of tweezers, as close to the skin as possible and twisting while pulling very gently but steadily. If pulled too abruptly, the head will remain in the skin where it will stay indefinitely, possibly causing a long-lasting swelling. Other methods often suggested include applying a drop of methylated spirits.

## ECZEMA AND MANGE
These terms are often very loosely and sometimes erroneously used. They (and any other skin trouble not obviously attributable to visible parasites) are best referred immediately to the vet.

## CANKER
This is another loosely used term, usually describing an accumulation of dirt and wax. Sometimes the trouble is due to mites (usually caught from cats). Shelties seldom suffer from these problems as their ears are not unduly hairy inside, and the semi-erect carriage allows plenty of ventilation. If necessary, the ear can be very carefully cleaned; never try to penetrate farther than you can see. If the area is obviously not encrusted by wax or dirt but is slightly damp-looking, a slight dusting of canker powder followed by gentle cleaning should help. The vet will advise you as to the type of powder to use, and will be able to help if this remedy does not work.

## INTERNAL PARASITES
Worms are parasites of infinite variety, affecting many living creatures and often dependent on a life-cycle involving more than one host, including man. Of the types known to affect dogs, the two most commonly encountered are the roundworm and the tapeworm.

## ROUNDWORMS
These are very commonly found in very young puppies and often in young adults.

They are the result of inadequate treatment in the puppy's youth or by reinfestation. They are not difficult to eliminate, and as remedies are constantly being improved and made safer, every puppy should have completed a full course of treatment before leaving for its new home at eight weeks or so. Piperazine-based remedies are safe and effective, provided they are given as directed. If in doubt, consult the vet, who will supply a suitable treatment

**TAPEWORMS**
Probably because of changes in the methods of feeding dogs, and because fleas (which play host to the tapeworm larvae) are more effectively treated, tapeworm are not nearly such a problem as they once were. Their presence is usually indicated by small, hard, grain-like particles which adhere to the hair round the dog's anus. These are dried segments of the worm which can be of astonishing length and which sheds segments from time to time. Unless its head is eradicated, it can continue to grow, so a specific remedy (obtainable from the vet) is required.

**HOOKWORMS**
These can cause acute debility because of their blood-sucking habit, but once identified they can be dealt with fairly easily.

**WHIPWORMS**
The same cannot be said of this elusive little parasite which inhabits the caecum, a blind sac at the end of the large intestine. Tucked away here, it is immune to any ordinary worm remedy which will go harmlessly past it. Once identified, it can be treated with a specific remedy, but it is important that this solution is found as soon as possible as the dysentery-like conditions it encourages can cause a dog to lose weight alarmingly.

**HEARTWORMS**
These are a serious problem with which American breeders have had to come to terms. Originally believed to be confined to the Southern States, these mosquito-borne pests have gradually spread northwards. They can have very serious effects, so they are best countered by preventative medication administered every day throughout the season when certain types of mosquito are active.

**HYDATOSIS**
This is a tapeworm-associated disease with a sheep/dog/man life-cycle. It exists in many parts of the world, but because of the paramount importance of the sheep industry in New Zealand its prevention and control is of great concern to that country. The importation of dogs into New Zealand is therefore subject to certified freedom from hydatid infection.

**TOXOCARIASIS**
In rare cases, the larva of the toxocara worm has been known to cause problems in the human body. This became the subject of much publicity, but the publicity failed to mention that the toxocara worm is carried not only by dogs, but also by cats and foxes. Anybody hesitating on this account to introduce a dog or cat into the household should consult a local vet, who will doubtless offer reassurance that the

*The Shetland Sheepdog is a hardy breed, and your dog should live a long and healthy life.*

*Good care and management are repaid – this twelve year-old Champion won his last Challenge Certificate at the age of eleven!*

risk would be minimal. It is worth remembering that those most at risk (breeders and others closely associated with domestic pets) are a remarkably healthy species!

At the same time, it must be pointed out that current unfavourable publicity directed against dogs, and the consequent restrictions on their freedom is a direct result of the carelessness and lack of consideration of previous generations of owners. Dog owners have an important part to play in the preservation of a pleasant environment and they have a duty to observe local legislation. It is quite unacceptable to allow dogs to foul either built-up areas or the open spaces from which they and their owners derive so much enjoyment.

## FIRST AID
It is obviously sensible to equip yourself with one or two useful items so that you can cope immediately with a first aid situation. Do not be tempted to hang on to out-of-date remedies, or you will soon accumulate a cupboard overflowing with leaky bottles, rusting tins or tattered envelopes containing crumbling antibiotic pills.

Apart from the fact that most forms of medication have a limited shelf-life, it is a great mistake to use, for example, the remains of a tube of eye ointment prescribed months ago, for a condition which seems identical. It may be quite different and to use the wrong remedy could do more harm than good.

## FIRST AID KIT
Useful items to keep in stock include:
A pair of scissors.
A few individually packed sterile dressings (preferably not the type embedded in elastoplast which could be very difficult to remove). Your vet may be able to supply these.
A roll of surgical tape (to keep dressings in place).
Antiseptic wound powder.
Antiseptic ointment.
A pack of tubegauze (or a type of bandaging which could be useful for a foot injury).
A bottle of Bitter Apple or some other deterrent to chewing or licking a wound or bandage.
A blunt-ended thermometer (a dog's normal temperature is 101.5 degrees F (38.5 degrees C). 104 degrees F must be considered high to the point of danger.

## WOUNDS
Minor cuts or grazes generally heal quickly after initial cleansing and a dusting of wound powder. Never use antiseptics or disinfectants at a greater strength than that recommended – it is better to err on the moderate side. Deep bites or more extensive wounds should be dealt with by the vet, as apart from the possible necessity for stitching, it is sometimes advisable to begin the healing process from within rather than from the surface.

## STINGS
It is always a good idea to carry a small phial of antihistamine tablets on walks or when going to shows etc. during the summer months, as dogs are often tempted to snap at bees or wasps, and the consequent stings in the mouth or on the tongue can cause alarming swellings which can be accompanied by shock as well as pain.

## DIARRHOEA

This is always a minor calamity in Shelties, as the evidence on a long-coated breed is very obvious! The usual cause of 'looseness' is over-rich, fatty food or simply over-eating. There is no point in persuading a dog in this condition to eat, but the next day you can feed a small meal of plain boiled chicken breast (not an expensive luxury these days) together with a diarrhoea pill. If, however, the diarrhoea is an unpleasant greyish or putty colour, accompanied by a foul smell it will require antibiotic treatment from the vet. Any sign of blood in faeces or vomit is also a matter for immediate veterinary treatment.

## HEREDITARY DISEASES

Most breeds are subject to certain hereditary conditions, and (as in humans) the number of identifiable diseases will increase as science continues to progress. In the case of dogs (though not in humans!) the main weapon used in eradicating hereditary problems is by the use of controlled breeding. Therefore, anybody considering breeding even one litter should be aware of the current problems and of the efforts being made to combat them.

The two diseases being specifically tackled in Shelties, at present, both concern eyes. The canine organisations involved with the breed have jointly evolved methods of testing appropriate to each condition. Your vet will give you more specific advice.

## PROGRESSIVE RETINAL ATROPHY (PRA)

PRA is a progressive and (at present) incurable eye disease which inevitably leads to blindness. Fortunately it is very rare in Shelties, but as one case would be one too many, it is vital that *every* dog used for breeding (even one litter) should be checked annually to ensure that it is currently free from PRA. The presence of this disease is not detectable at birth; its progress is gradual, and the condition may already be well advanced before the owner realises that something is amiss. This is seldom evident until the dog is at least two years old – generally it will be even older, so it may already have been used for breeding, possibly doing untold harm.

It is therefore essential that every animal (dog or bitch) used for breeding should be examined annually. A copy of the certificate will be handed to the owner, another being sent to the owner's vet, and further copies to the official organising bodies. Although the condition will progress to total blindness, the outlook for the individual dog is not quite as tragic as might be imagined, provided it continues to live in a familiar environment. The process is very gradual, and as a dog relies as much on its sense of smell as on its sight, it will manage very well on its home ground, given care and understanding. The importance of controlling this disease is, however, obvious.

## COLLIE EYE ANOMALY (CEA)

Here, the situation is much less discouraging than PRA, as CEA is present at birth, and it can be diagnosed by an expert between the ages of five and eight weeks old. It is therefore feasible (at the expenditure of a good deal of effort!) to have whole litters of puppies examined before they are dispersed to their new homes.

Generally, puppies not passed as 'clear' are likely to be only so mildly affected that they will never suffer any inconvenience or loss of vision. Very occasionally, more severely affected dogs may suffer from a detached retina or from intra-ocular

*There has been a steady improvement in the number of puppies born free of hereditary eye problems, thanks to regular testing of breeding stock.*

haemorrhage, in which case blindness could occur in the affected eye. This occurs very rarely and the mildly affected dog can almost certainly look forward to a long and happy life, quite unaware that he hasn't a 'clear' certificate!

The reason that the condition is being so closely monitored is that when originally diagnosed in the breed it was already so widespread (about 80 per cent of Shelties examined were affected) that had no steps been taken to check its incidence, it might have spread throughout the breed. Breeding from only affected dogs, we might eventually have found that the number of serious cases would have become progressively greater.

The efforts made over fifteen years or so have enabled those breeders participating in the testing scheme to adapt their breeding plans so as to achieve a steady improvement in the percentage of 'clear' puppies produced, and to increase the number (very low at present) of genetically clear dogs, who could speed progress quite dramatically in the future.

## HIP DYSPLASIA

Thanks to its fairly light build and to a sensible Breed Standard requirement for structure, i.e. balanced and free from any exaggerations, hip dysplasia has never been a major problem in Shetland Sheepdogs. However, cases have been diagnosed from time to time, and as it is an hereditary disease (although with environmental connections) it must not be ignored. It can be very slight, or extremely painful to the point of immobilizing the dog. There is an official scheme for the diagnosis of hip dysplasia involving X-ray examination under anaesthesia.